M000119740

First edition December 2012

Published by Design Community College Inc,

Design Community College Inc.
PO Box 1153
Topanga CA 90290 USA

info@curedale.com
Designed and illustrated by Robert Curedale

Cover Image: Copyright 2012 echo3005,
Used under license from Shutterstock.com

ISBN-13: 978-0-9882362-19

ISBN-10: 0988236214

Structured Workshops
The author presents workshops online and
in person in global locations for executives,
engineers, designers, technology professionals
and anyone interested in learning and applying
these proven innovation methods. For
information contact: info@curedale.com

Design Methods 2

200 more ways to apply design thinking

Robert Curedale

dgh

Dedication

Dedicated to nancy, ward, gail and john

introduction

This is the second volume in the Design Methods series. The two volumes together cover 400 methods and are the most extensive collection of design methods available. The methods can be applied by designers and professionals working in design teams in all areas of design and architecture. These are tools to support a trend in most areas of design towards a methods based approach.

The trend is a necessary evolution in the way that design is being done for the many situations in which traditional design skills are not adequate to find the best solution to a design problem. These methods are becoming required skills for designers everywhere. The methods described have been tested and successfully applied across disciplines, across cultures, across the globe. They will enable you to design products, systems buildings, interfaces and experiences with confidence that you have created the most informed design solutions for real people that is possible. We believe that this is the largest collection of design methods that is available and with the companion volume two is an indispensable resource for anyone practicing design.

Traditional design methods equip designers to design the aesthetic qualities of objects, graphics and other physical or digital expressions of design. Designers today are being asked to design these things as integral parts of more complex systems of services and experiences.

These methods allow a designer to balance both analytical and creative thinking processes concurrently and to work effectively as a member of a cross disciplinary design team.

The structure of Western economies has changed over the last five decades. There has been a steady increase in employment in the service sector and a steady decrease of employment in manufacturing as technologies such as robotics replaced labor in factories. In the United States the service sector now employs 90% of the working population. This has risen from around 50% in 1960. Organizations that employ designers need to create design that balances the requirements of complex ecosystems of products, environments, services and experiences both physical and virtual. Traditional design skills such as drawing are effective ways of communicating three dimensional forms and two dimensional graphic design but are not able to describe the forth dimension necessary in service and experience design which is time. Services and experiences change over time.

When a designer is asked to design a product, environment or service for a chain of coffee shops, the designer must consider a complex interaction of products, services, people, business, technology environments and architecture. A designer faces a similar problem when designing a product or service for a multinational corporation. The designer must consider the complex relationships of many products, services, people and environments in order to define a single product.

Traditional design education has cast a designer as a type of artist who essentially works alone and places personal self expression above all else. The methods stress design as a collaborative activity where designers respect and have empathy for the other development team members and where design is informed by an understanding of the perspectives of the people who will eventually use the finished design.

The methods in these volumes balance both modes of thinking so that designers can contribute effectively in both the divergent or idea generation phases of design and the convergent or defining and refining phases of design. The methods allow a designer to create informed design with logical justifications for their decisions that can be communicated convincingly to managers, engineers and financial people. I have kept the descriptions simple to give readers the essential information to adapt, combine and apply the methods in their own way. I hope that you will gradually build a personal toolkit of favored methods that you have tried and found effective. Different design practitioners can select different methods for their toolkit and apply them in different ways. There is no best combination.

contents

Chapter 1
Thinking approaches   1

Design Thinking   3
Critical Thinking   10

Chapter 2
Team Building Exercises   15

Team Building Exercises   17
    Common ground   19
    Diversity   20
    Expectations   21
    Looking Back   22
    Milestones   23
    Names   24
    Places   25
    Time Machine   26

Chapter 3
Defining the vision   27

3p analysis   29
7p's   31
Action plan   33
Appreciative inquiry   35
Assumption surfacing   37
Bhag   39
Boundary examination   41
Bowman's strategy clock   43
Checklists   45
    Environment   46
    Reality check   47
    Product design brief   49
    Web design brief   50
Clarkson ethics principles   51
Critical success factor   53
Decision rings   55

Dialectical inquiry   57
Force field analysis   59
Future wheel   61
Go and no go   63
Goal grid   65
Goal orientation   67
Heptalysis   69
Is is not   71
Kaizen method   73
Reframing the problem   74
Kepner tregoe analysis   75
Key performance indicator   77
Kick off meeting   79
Likert scale   81
Meeting evaluation   83
Mirror   85
Mission statement   87
Moscow prioritization   89
Most analysis   91
CATWOE   92
Multivoting   93
Octagon   95
Ohmae 3c model   97
PESTLE   99
Polarities matrix   101
Powergram   103
Premortem   105
Requirements catalog   107
Risk map   109
Risk reward analysis   111
Rotating roles   113
Semantic intuition   115
Shredded questions   117
Stakeholder scope map   119
Trajectories of change   121
VPEC-T   123

Chapter 4
Know people and context

Chapter 4
Know people and context   125

Active listening   127
Activity analysis   129
Anthropometric analysis   131
Anthropump   133
Autoethnography   135
Blind trials
    Single blind   137
    Double blind   138
Case Studies
    Clinical   139
    Historical   141
    Multi case   143
    Observational   145
    Oral history   147
    Situational   149
Close ended questions   151
Conjoint analysis   153
Customer first questions   155
Customer needs matrix   157
Deming cycle   159
Dramaturgy   161
Drawing experiences   163
Ethnocentrism   165
Explore represent share   167
Field experiment   169
Focus groups
    Client participant   171
    Devil's advocate   172
    Dual moderator   173
    Mini focus group   174
    Online focus group   175
    Other participant   176
    Respondent moderator   177
    Structured focus group   178
    Teleconference   179

Two way   180
Unstructured   181
Focus troupe   182
Idiographic approach   183
Innovation diagnostic   185
Interviews
    Naturalistic group   187
    Photo elicitation   189
Method bank   191
Nomothetic approach   193
Hawthorne effect   195
Object stimulation   197
Observation methods
    Covert   199
    Direct   201
    Indirect   202
    Non participant   203
    Participant   204
    Overt   205
    Structured   207
    Unstructured   208
Online methods   209
    Ethnography   210
    Clinical trials   211
    Focus groups   212
    Interviews   213
    Questionnaires   214
    Experiments   215
    Online ethics   216
Open ended questions   217
Placebo controlled study   219
Sampling methods
    Cluster   221
    Convenience   223
    Random   224
    Expert   225
    Situation   227
    Stratified   229

Systematic 230
Sampling: Time 231
Sociogram 233

Chapter 5
Frame insights 235

Bar chart 237
Bullet proofing 239
Comparative matrix 241
Delphi method 243
Dot diagram 245
Feature permutation 247
Gozinto chart 249
Line chart 251
Linking diagram 253
Maslow's hierarchy of needs 255
Pictogram 257
Pie chart 259
Process flow diagram 261
Product lifecycle map 263
Visual dissonance 265

Chapter 6
Explore ideas 267

10x10 sketch method 269
Alexander's method 271
Attribute analysis 272
Brainstorming
    Analogies and metaphors 273
    Benjamin Franklin method 275
    Crawford slip method 277
    Disney method 278
    Greeting cards 279
    Nominal group method 281
    Out of the box 283
    Pin cards 285
    Pool method 287
    Post-it 289
    Rolestorming 291
    Starbusting 292
    STP method 293
    Up and down 295
    Wishful thinking 297
Business matrix analysis 299
Cluster analysis 301
Collective notebook 303
Competencies model 305
Consensus decision making 307
Convergent thinking 309
Divergent thinking 311
Countermeasures matrix 313
Creative problem solving process 315
Group circle 316
Double reversal 317
Gunning fog index 319
Heuristic ideation 321
Idea advocate 323
Information market 324
Matchett's design method 325

Morphological analysis   321
Page's strategy   329
Pattern language   330
Pearson's method   331
Phillips 66 method   333
Productive thinking model   335
Reframing matrix   337
Rich pictures   339
Secret voting   340
Simplex method   341
Small groups   343
Sociodrama   344
Strategy switching   345
Vroom yetton decision model   347
Word diamond   349

Chapter 7   **351**
Prototype and iterate

a/b testing   353
Generative prototyping   355
Dark horse prototype   357
Pictive   359
Appearance prototype   360

Templates   **361**

Action plan   363
Comparative matrix   364
Decision rings   365
Goal grid   366
Heptalysis   367
Meeting evaluation   368
Multivoting score sheet   369
Polarities matrix   370
Risk reward analysis   371
Risk Map   372
Reframing matrix   373
Word diamond   374

Index   **375**

Other titles in this series, Workshops **385**

About the author   **386**

Chapter 1
Thinking Approaches

design thinking

WHAT IS IT?

Design Thinking is a methodology or approach to designing that should help you be more consistently innovative. It involves methods that enable empathy with people, it focuses on people. It is a collaborative methodology that involves iterative prototyping. It involves a series of divergent and convergent phases. It combines analytical and creative thinking approaches. It involves a toolkit of methods that can be applied to different styles of problems by different types of people. Anyone can use Design Thinking. It can be fun.

WHO INVENTED IT?

The origins of new design methods date back to before the 1950s. 1987 Peter Rowe, Professor at the Harvard Graduate School of Design, published "Design Thinking" the first significant usage of the term "Design Thinking" in literature. After 2000 the term became widely used.

CHALLENGES

1. There has been little research to validate claims about Design Thinking by advocates.
2. Some critics of Design Thinking suggest that it is a successful attempt to brand a set of existing concepts and frameworks with a appealing idea.

WHY USE DESIGN THINKING?

Design Thinking is useful when you have:
1. A poorly defined problem.
2. A lack of information.
3. A changing context or environment
4. It should result in consistently innovative solutions.

Design Thinking seeks a balance of design considerations including:
1. Business.
2. Empathy with people.
3. Application of technologies.
4. Environmental consideration.

Design Thinking seeks to balance two modes of thinking:
1. Analytical thinking
2. Creative Thinking

Advocates of Design Thinking believe that the approach results in consistently innovative design solutions oriented towards people.

Design Thinking takes a cross disciplinary team approach. It rejects the idea of a designer being a lone expert artist working in a studio remote from people in favor of an approach where a designer collaborates with a multidisciplinary team. Design Thinking advocates making informed decisions based on evidence gathered from the people and context in place of designers working on a hunch.

WHEN TO USE DESIGN THINKING

Design Thinking is an approach that can be applied throughout the design process:

1. Define intent
2. Know Context
3. Know User
4. Frame insights
5. Explore Concepts
6. Make Plans
7. Deliver Offering

RESOURCES

1. Paper
2. Pens
3. Camera
4. Notebook
5. Post-it-notes
6. Cardboard
7. White board
8. Dry-erase markers

REFERENCES

1. Martin, Roger L. The Opposable Mind: How Successful Leaders Win through Integrative Thinking. Boston, MA: Harvard Business School, 2007.
2. Buchanan, Richard, "Wicked Problems in Design Thinking," Design Issues, vol. 8, no. 2, Spring 1992
3. Cross, Nigel. "Designerly Ways of Knowing." Design Studies 3.4 (1982): 221-27.
4. Brown, Tim, and Katz, Barry. Change by Design: How Design Thinking Transforms Organizations and Inspires Innovation. New York: Harper Business, 2009.
5. Florida, Richard L. The Rise of the Creative Class: and How It is Transforming Work, Leisure, Community and Everyday Life. New York, NY: Basic, 2002 Basic, 2002
6. Jones, John Christopher. Design Methods. New York: John Wiley & Sons, 1970.

design thinking

FOCUS ON PEOPLE:

Design is more about people than it is about things. It is important to stand in those people's shoes, to see through their eyes, to uncover their stories, to share their worlds. Start each design by identifying a problem that real people are experiencing. Use the methods in this book selectively to gain empathy and understanding. and to inform your design. Good process is not a substitute for talented and skilled people on your design team.

GET PHYSICAL

Make simple physical prototypes of your ideas as early as possible. Constantly test your ideas with people. Do not worry about making prototypes beautiful until you are sure that you have a resolved final design. Use the prototypes to guide and improve your design. Do a lot of low cost prototypes to test how Your Ideas physically work. using cardboard, paper, markers, adhesive tape, photocopies, string and popsicle sticks. The idea is to test your idea, not to look like the final product. Expect to change it again. Limit your costs to ten or twenty dollars. Iterate, test and iterate. Do not make the prototype jewelry. It can stand in the way of finding the best design solution. In the minds of some a high fidelity prototype is a finished design solution rather than a tool for improving a design. You should make your idea physical as soon as possible. Be the first to get your hands dirty by making the idea real.

BE CURIOUS

Ask why? Explore and Experiment. Go outside your comfort zone. Do not assume that you know the answer. Look for inspiration in new ways and places. Christopher Columbus and Albert Einstein followed their curiosity to new places.

SEEK TEAM DIVERSITY

A diverse design team will produce more successful design than a team that lacks diversity. Innovation needs a collision of different ideas and approaches. Your team should have different genders, different ages, be from different cultures, different socioeconomic backgrounds and have different outlooks to be most successful. With diversity expect some conflict. Manage conflict productively and the best ideas will float to the surface. Have team members who have lived in different countries and cultures and with global awareness. Cross cultural life experience enables people to be more creative.

TAKE CONSIDERED RISKS

Taking considered risks is helps create differentiated design. Many designers and organizations do not have the flexibility or courage to create innovative, differentiated design solutions so they create products and services that are like existing products and services and must compete on price.
"It takes a lot of courage to release the familiar and seemingly secure, to embrace the new, but there is no real security in what is no longer meaningful. There is more security in the adventurous and exciting, for in movement there is life, and in change, there is power."
Alan Cohen

USE THE TOOLS

To understand the point of view of diverse peoples and cultures a designer needs to connect with those people and their context. The tools in this book are an effective way of seeing the world through the eyes of those people.

LEARN TO SEE AND HEAR

Reach out to understand people. Interpret what you see and hear. Read between the lines. Make new connections between the things you see and hear.

COMBINE ANALYTICAL AND CREATIVE THINKING

Effective collaboration is part of effective design. Designers work like members of an orchestra. We need to work with managers, engineers, salespeople and other professions. Human diversity and life experience contribute to better design solutions.

LOOK FOR BALANCE

Design Thinking seeks a balance of design factors including:

1. Business.
2. Empathy with people.
3. Application OF technology.
4. Environmental consideration.

TEAM COLLABORATION

Design today is a more complex activity than it was in the past. Business, technology, global cultural issues, environmental considerations, and human considerations all need careful consideration. Design Thinking recognizes the need for designers to be working as members of multidisciplinary multi skilled teams.

The need for creative self expression for designers is important. For an artist the need for creative self expression is a primary need. For a designer this need must be balanced by an awareness and response to the needs of others. Balanced design needs analytical as well as creative thinking. The methods in this book balance a designer's creative thinking with analytical thinking. This balance comes most effectively from a team rather than from an individual. Designers must respond to the needs of the design team, the needs of the business needs of those who employ us to design and the needs of those people that we design for.

design thinking process

DEFINE THE VISION?
What are we looking for?

1. Meet with key stakeholders to set vision
2. Assemble a diverse team
3. Develop intent and vision
4. Explore scenarios of user experience
5. Document user performance requirements
6. Define the group of people you are designing for. What is their gender, age, and income range. Where do they live. What is their culture?
7. Define your scope and constraints
8. Identify a need that you are addressing. Identify a problem that you are solving.
9. Identify opportunities
10. Meet stakeholders

KNOW THE PEOPLE AND CONTEXT
What else is out there?

1. Identify what you know and what you need to know.
2. Document a research plan
3. Benchmark competitive products
4. Create a budgeting and plan.
5. Create tasks and deliverables
6. Explore the context of use
7. Understand the risks
8. Observe and interview individuals, groups, experts.
9. Develop design strategy
10. Undertake qualitative, quantitative, primary and secondary research.
11. Talk to vendors

EXPLORE IDEAS
How is this for starters?

1. Brainstorm
2. Define the most promising ideas
3. Refine the ideas
4. Establish key differentiation of your ideas
5. Investigate existing intellectual property.

PROTOTYPE TEST AND ITERATE
How could we make it better?

1. Make your favored ideas physical.
2. Create low-fidelity prototypes from inexpensive available materials
3. Develop question guides
4. Develop test plan
5. Test prototypes with stakeholders
6. Get feedback from people.
7. Refine the prototypes
8. Test again
9. Build in the feedback
10. Refine again.
11. Continue iteration until design works.
12. Document the process.
13. When you are confident that your idea works make a prototype that looks and works like a production product.

DELIVER
Let's make it. Let's sell it.

1. Create your proposed production design
2. Test and evaluate
3. Review objectives
4. Manufacture your first samples
5. Review first production samples and refine.
6. Launch
7. Obtain user feedback
8. Conduct field studies
9. Define the vision for the next product or service.

critical thinking

WHAT IS IT?
Critical thinking is the discipline of rigorously and skillfully using information, experience, observation and reasoning to guide your decisions, actions and beliefs.

WHO INVENTED IT?
Socrates, Buddhist kalama sutta and Abhidharma.

WHY USE THIS METHOD?
1. More effective decisions
2. More efficient use of time
3. Rational rather than emotion-driven decisions.

WHEN TO USE THIS METHOD
1. Define intent
2. Know Context
3. Know User
4. Frame insights
5. Explore Concepts
6. Make Plans
7. Deliver Offering

HOW TO USE THIS METHOD
Critical thinking skills include:
1. Recognizing and solving problems.
2. Information gathering.
3. Interpreting information.
4. Recognizing relationships.
5. Drawing sound conclusions.
6. Leaning from experience
7. Recognizing assumptions.
8. Self criticism.
9. Self awareness.
10. Reflective thought.
11. Understanding meaning.

REFERENCES
1. Title: Critical Thinking Handbook: K-3rd Grades. A Guide for Remodelling Lesson Plans in Language Arts, Social Studies, and Science. Author: Richard W. Paul, A.J.A. Binker, Daniel Weil. Publisher: Foundation for Critical Thinking. ISBN: 0-944583-05-9
2. Paul, Richard; and Elder, Linda. The Miniature Guide to Critical Thinking Concepts and Tools. Dillon Beach: Foundation for Critical Thinking Press, 2008, p. 4. ISBN 978-0-944583-10-4
3. Ennis, R.H., "Critical Thinking Assessment" in Fasko, Critical Thinking and Reasoning: Current Research, Theory, and Practice (2003). ISBN 978-1-57273-460-9

critical thinking

"Critical thinking is independent thinking for oneself. Many of our beliefs are acquired at an early age, when we have a strong tendency to form beliefs for irrational reasons (because we want to believe, because we are praised or rewarded for believing). Critical thinkers use critical skills and insights to reveal and reject beliefs that are irrational.

In forming new beliefs, critical thinkers do not passively accept the beliefs of others; rather, they try to figure things out for themselves.

They are not limited by accepted ways of doing things. They evaluate both goals and how to achieve them. They do not accept as true, or reject as false, beliefs they do not understand. They are not easily manipulated."

Source: The critical thinking Handbook. Richard W. Paul

AFFECTIVE STRATEGIES

1. Thinking independently
2. Developing insight into egocentricity or sociocentricity
3. Exercising fair-mindedness
4. Exploring thoughts underlying feelings and feelings underlying thoughts
5. Developing intellectual humility and suspending judgment
6. Developing intellectual courage
7. Developing intellectual good faith or integrity
8. Developing intellectual perseverance
9. Developing confidence in reason

Source: The critical thinking Handbook. Richard W. Paul

COGNITIVE STRATEGIES MACRO-ABILITIES

1. Refining generalizations and avoiding oversimplifications
2. Comparing analogous situations: transferring insights to new contexts
3. Developing one's perspective: creating or exploring beliefs, arguments, or theories
4. Clarifying issues, conclusions, or beliefs
5. Clarifying and analyzing the meanings of words or phrases
6. Developing criteria for evaluation: clarifying values and standards
7. Evaluating the credibility of sources of information
8. Questioning deeply: raising and pursuing root or significant questions
9. Analyzing or evaluating arguments, interpretations, beliefs, or theories
10. Generating or assessing solutions
11. Analyzing or evaluating actions or policies
12. Reading critically: clarifying or critiquing texts
13. Listening critically: the art of silent dialogue
14. Making interdisciplinary connections
15. Practicing Socratic discussion: clarifying and questioning beliefs, theories, or perspectives
16. Reasoning dialogically: comparing perspectives, interpretations, or theories
17. Reasoning dialectically: evaluating perspectives, interpretations, or theories

Source: The critical thinking Handbook. Richard W. Paul

COGNITIVE STRATEGIES MICRO-ABILITIES

1. Comparing and contrasting ideals with actual practice
2. Thinking precisely about thinking: using critical vocabulary
3. Noting significant similarities and differences
4. Examining or evaluating assumptions
5. Distinguishing relevant from irrelevant facts
6. Making plausible inferences, predictions, or interpretations
7. Giving reasons and evaluating evidence and alleged facts
8. Recognizing contradictions
9. Exploring implications and consequences

Source: The critical thinking Handbook. Richard W. Paul

teaching critical thinking

STRATEGIES

1. Urge students to be reflective
2. Ask such questions as "How do you know", and "Is that a good source of information?"
3. Explore conclusions, explanations, sources of evidence, points of view
4. Discuss problems in the context of realistic situations that students see as significant
5. Ask "Why?"
6. Emphasize seeing things from others' points of view
7. Students do not need to become subject-matter experts before they can start to learn to think critically in a subject
8. Ask students to address questions to which you do not know the answer, or that are controversial. The question should seem significant to them and be interesting
9. Have them work on issues or questions in groups, with each group reporting to the entire class, and each person showing the others what he or she has done.

Source: Robert H. Ennis and Sean F. Ennis.

FRISCO

When appraising a position, whether yours or another's, attend at least to these elements:

1. F for Focus: Identify or be clear about the main point, that is, the conclusion
2. R for Reasons: Identify and evaluate the reasons
3. I for Inference: Consider whether the reasons establish the conclusion, given the alternatives
4. S for Situation: Pay attention to the situation
5. C for Clarity: Make sure that the meanings are clear
6. O for Overview: Review your entire appraisal as a unit

ABILITIES
Critical thinkers:
Care that their beliefs be true and that their decisions be justified;

- Seek alternative hypotheses, explanations, conclusions, plans, sources, etc.; and be open to them
- Consider seriously other points of view than their own
- Try to be well informed
- Endorse a position to the extent that, but only to the extent that, it is justified by the information that is available
- Use their critical thinking abilities

Care to understand and present a position honestly and clearly, theirs as well as others'; including to

- Discover and listen to others' view and reasons
- Be clear about the intended meaning of what is said, written, or otherwise communicated, seeking as much precision as the situation requires
- Determine, and maintain focus on, the conclusion or question
- Seek and offer reasons
- Take into account the total situation
- Be reflectively aware of their own basic beliefs

Care about every person. Caring critical thinkers

- Avoid intimidating or confusing others with their critical thinking prowess, taking into account others' feelings and level of understanding
- Are concerned about others' welfare

Source: Robert H. Ennis and Sean F. Ennis.

REFERENCES
1. Sobocan, Jan & Groarke, Leo (Eds.), (2009), Critical thinking education and assessment: Can higher order thinking be tested? London, Ontario: Althouse Press.
2. Possin, Kevin (2008). A guide to critical thinking assessment.
3. CRITICAL THINKING Robert H. Ennis1996, Upper Saddle River, NJ: Prentice-Hall ISBN: 0-13-374711-5
4. HOW TO THINK LOGICALLY Gary Seay & Susana Nuccetelli 2008, 592 pgs. Pearson Higher Education ISBN 0321337778

Chapter 2
Team Building Exercises
get to know the team

team building exercises

WHAT IS IT?

An icebreaker is a short exercise at the beginning of a design project that helps the design team work productively together as quickly as possible. The duration of an icebreaker is usually less than 30 minutes.

They are an important component of collaborative or team based design. The Design Thinking approach recognizes the value of designers working productively as members of a diverse cross-disciplinary teams with managers, engineers, marketers and other professionals.

WHY USE THIS METHOD?

When a designer works with others in a new team it is important that the group works as quickly as possible in a creative constructive dialogue. An icebreaker is a way for team members to quickly start working effectively;y together. It is a worthwhile investment of half an hour at the beginning of a project and can be fun. Ice breakers help start people thinking creatively, exchanging ideas and help make a team work effectively. For meetings in a business setting in which contribute.

WHEN USE THIS METHOD

1. When team members do not know each other
2. When team members come from different cultures
3. When team needs to bond quickly
4. When team needs to work to a common gaol quickly.
5. When the discussion is new or unfamiliar.
6. When the moderator needs to know the participants.

common ground

WHAT IS IT?

An ice-breaker is an exercise that is used at the beginning of a design project or workshop to help to stimulate constructive interaction. It helps everyone to engage in the dialogue and contribute effectively,

WHY USE THIS METHOD?

1. Helps create a comfortable and productive environment.
2. Helps people get to know each other.
3. Helps participants engage the group and tasks.
4. Helps participants contribute effectively.
5. Creates a sense of community.

CHALLENGES

1. Be aware of time constraints.
2. Should limit the time to 15 to 30 minutes
3. Make it simple
4. It should be fun
5. You should be creative
6. Be enthusiastic
7. If something isn't working move on.
8. Consider your audience
9. Keep in mind technology requirements such as a microphone or projector.
10. Chairs can be arranged in a circle to help participants read body language.
11. Select exercises appropriate for your group.

WHEN TO USE THIS METHOD

1. Define intent

HOW TO USE THIS METHOD

1. The moderator ask the group to divide into pairs of participants
2. Each participant should select a group member that they do not know if possible.
3. Each person should interview the other person that they are paired with and make a list of 5 to ten things that they have in common.
4. One person from each pair should then present the list to the larger group.

RESOURCES

1. White board
2. Dry erase markers
3. A comfortable space

REFERENCES

1. Fergueson, S., & Aimone, L. (2002). Making people feel valued. Communication: Journalism Education Today, 36(1), 5-11
2. Sisco, B. R. (1991). Setting the climate for effective teaching and learning. New Directions for Adult and Continuing Education, (50), 41-50.
3. Sisco, B. R. (1991). Setting the climate for effective teaching and learning. New Directions for Adult and Continuing Education, (50), 41-50.

diversity

WHAT IS IT?

An ice-breaker is an exercise that is used at the beginning of a design project or workshop to help to stimulate constructive interaction. It helps everyone to engage in the dialogue and contribute effectively,

WHY USE THIS METHOD?

1. Helps create a comfortable and productive environment.
2. Helps people get to know each other.
3. Helps participants engage the group and tasks.
4. Helps participants contribute effectively.
5. Creates a sense of community.

CHALLENGES

1. Be aware of time constraints.
2. Should limit the time to 15 to 30 minutes
3. Make it simple
4. It should be fun
5. You should be creative
6. Be enthusiastic
7. If something isn't working move on.
8. Consider your audience
9. Keep in mind technology requirements such as a microphone or projector.
10. Chairs can be arranged in a circle to help participants read body language.
11. Select exercises appropriate for your group.

WHEN TO USE THIS METHOD

1. Define intent

HOW TO USE THIS METHOD

2. The moderator introduces the exercise.
3. Place a number of objects or cards on the floor that represent the relative positions of the continents on a map of the earth.
4. The moderator asks each person to move to the spot where they were born.
5. When the group is in position the moderator asks each person to tell the group one thing about the place they were born.
6. Allow one or two minutes per person.
7. When this is complete the moderator asks the group to move to the place where they have spent the most of their adult life and tell the group one thing about that place.

RESOURCES

1. White board
2. Dry erase markers
3. A large comfortable space

REFERENCES

1. Fergueson, S., & Aimone, L. (2002). Making people feel valued. Communication: Journalism Education Today, 36(1), 5-11
2. Sisco, B. R. (1991). Setting the climate for effective teaching and learning. New Directions for Adult and Continuing Education, (50), 41-50.
3. Sisco, B. R. (1991). Setting the climate for effective teaching and learning.

expectations

WHAT IS IT?
An ice-breaker is an exercise that is used at the beginning of a design project or workshop to help to stimulate constructive interaction. It helps everyone to engage in the dialogue and contribute effectively,

WHY USE THIS METHOD?
1. Helps create a comfortable and productive environment.
2. Helps people get to know each other.
3. Helps participants engage the group and tasks.
4. Helps participants contribute effectively.
5. Creates a sense of community.

CHALLENGES
1. Be aware of time constraints. Should limit the time to 15 to 30 minutes
2. Make it simple
3. It should be fun
4. You should be creative
5. Be enthusiastic
6. If something isn't working move on.
7. Consider your audience
8. Keep in mind technology requirements such as a microphone or projector.
9. Chairs can be arranged in a circle to help participants read body language.
10. Select exercises appropriate for your group.

WHEN TO USE THIS METHOD
1. Define intent

HOW TO USE THIS METHOD
1. Each team member introduces themselves
2. Each team member outlines what is their expectations of the project.
3. Each team member shares their vision of the best possible outcome for the project.
4. Allow about 2 minutes per person

RESOURCES
1. White board
2. Dry erase markers
3. A comfortable space

REFERENCES
1. Fergueson, S., & Aimone, L. (2002). Making people feel valued. Communication: Journalism Education Today, 36(1), 5-11
2. Sisco, B. R. (1991). Setting the climate for effective teaching and learning. New Directions for Adult and Continuing Education, (50), 41-50.

looking back

WHAT IS IT?
An ice-breaker is an exercise that is used at the beginning of a design project or workshop to help to stimulate constructive interaction. It helps everyone to engage in the dialogue and contribute effectively,

WHY USE THIS METHOD?
1. Helps create a comfortable and productive environment.
2. Helps people get to know each other.
3. Helps participants engage the group and tasks.
4. Helps participants contribute effectively.
5. Creates a sense of community.

CHALLENGES
1. Be aware of time constraints.
2. Should limit the time to 15 to 30 minutes
3. Make it simple
4. It should be fun
5. You should be creative
6. Be enthusiastic
7. If something isn't working move on.
8. Consider your audience
9. Keep in mind technology requirements such as a microphone or projector.
10. Chairs can be arranged in a circle to help participants read body language.
11. Select exercises appropriate for your group.

WHEN TO USE THIS METHOD
1. Define intent

HOW TO USE THIS METHOD
1. Divide people into groups of 4 people.
2. The moderator asks the group to imagine that it is the last day of the project.
3. Ask each person to imagine what they got out of the project and what the project has achieved and to explain it to their group of 4.
4. Each group selects the most interesting story and a spokesperson for the group.
5. The group spokespeople present the most interesting story for their group to the larger group.

RESOURCES
1. White board
2. Dry erase markers
3. A comfortable space

REFERENCES
1. Fergueson, S., & Aimone, L. (2002). Making people feel valued. Communication: Journalism Education Today, 36(1), 5-11
2. Sisco, B. R. (1991). Setting the climate for effective teaching and learning. New Directions for Adult and Continuing Education, (50), 41-50.

milestones

WHAT IS IT?

An ice-breaker is an exercise that is used at the beginning of a design project or workshop to help to stimulate constructive interaction. It helps everyone to engage in the dialogue and contribute effectively,

WHO INVENTED IT?

Ava S, Butler 1996

WHY USE THIS METHOD?

1. Helps create a comfortable and productive environment.
2. Helps people get to know each other.
3. Helps participants engage the group and tasks.
4. Helps participants contribute effectively.
5. Creates a sense of community.

CHALLENGES

1. Be aware of time constraints.
2. Should limit the time to 15 to 30 minutes
3. Make it simple
4. It should be fun
5. You should be creative
6. Be enthusiastic
7. If something isn't working move on.
8. Consider your audience
9. Keep in mind technology requirements such as a microphone or projector.
10. Chairs can be arranged in a circle to help participants read body language.
11. Select exercises appropriate for your group.

WHEN TO USE THIS METHOD

1. Define intent

HOW TO USE THIS METHOD

1. The moderator creates a milestone chart on a white board
2. The moderator estimates the age of the oldest members of the group and on a horizontal line write years from the approximate birth year of the older members to the present at 5 year intervals.
1960 1965 1970 1975 .
3. Using post-it notes each participant adds three personal milestones to the chart. One milestone per post-it-note under the year that the milestone occurred.
4. During the break participants read the milestones.

RESOURCES

5. Whiteboard
6. Dry erase markers
7. Post-it-notes
8. A comfortable space

REFERENCES

1. Butler, Ava S. (1996) Teamthink Publisher: Mcgraw Hill ISBN 0070094330

23

names

WHAT IS IT?

An ice-breaker is an exercise that is used at the beginning of a design project or workshop to help to stimulate constructive interaction. It helps everyone to engage in the dialogue and contribute effectively,

WHY USE THIS METHOD?

1. Helps create a comfortable and productive environment.
2. Helps people get to know each other.
3. Helps participants engage the group and tasks.
4. Helps participants contribute effectively.
5. Creates a sense of community.

CHALLENGES

1. Be aware of time constraints.
2. Should limit the time to 15 to 30 minutes
3. Make it simple
4. It should be fun
5. You should be creative
6. Be enthusiastic
7. If something isn't working move on.
8. Consider your audience
9. Keep in mind technology requirements such as a microphone or projector.
10. Chairs can be arranged in a circle to help participants read body language.
11. Select exercises appropriate for your group.

WHEN TO USE THIS METHOD

1. Define intent

HOW TO USE THIS METHOD

1. Divide people into groups of 4 people.
2. Ask each person to tell their group the story of their first and second name.
3. Allow 3 minutes per person.
4. Each group selects the most interesting story and a spokesperson for the group.
5. The group spokespeople present the most interesting story for their group to the larger group.

RESOURCES

1. White board
2. Dry erase markers
3. A comfortable space

REFERENCES

1. Fergueson, S., & Aimone, L. (2002). Making people feel valued. Communication: Journalism Education Today, 36(1), 5-11
2. Sisco, B. R. (1991). Setting the climate for effective teaching and learning. New Directions for Adult and Continuing Education, (50), 41-50.

places

WHAT IS IT?

An ice-breaker is an exercise that is used at the beginning of a design project or workshop to help to stimulate constructive interaction. It helps everyone to engage in the dialogue and contribute effectively,

WHY USE THIS METHOD?

1. Helps create a comfortable and productive environment.
2. Helps people get to know each other.
3. Helps participants engage the group and tasks.
4. Helps participants contribute effectively.
5. Creates a sense of community.

CHALLENGES

1. Be aware of time constraints. Should limit the time to 15 to 30 minutes
2. Make it simple
3. It should be fun
4. You should be creative
5. Be enthusiastic
6. If something isn't working move on.
7. Consider your audience
8. Keep in mind technology requirements such as a microphone or projector.
9. Chairs can be arranged in a circle to help participants read body language.
10. Select exercises appropriate for your group.

WHEN TO USE THIS METHOD

1. Define intent

HOW TO USE THIS METHOD

1. Each team member introduces themselves
2. Ask each team members to give three clues to a place that they are from, have been to or want to go to.
3. Give the team a few minutes.
4. Each team member takes two minutes to describe the clues. Other members of the group guess the location.
5. The member describing the location reveals the location and describes it

RESOURCES

1. White board
2. Dry erase markers
3. A comfortable space

REFERENCES

1. Fergueson, S., & Aimone, L. (2002). Making people feel valued. Communication: Journalism Education Today, 36(1), 5-11
2. Sisco, B. R. (1991). Setting the climate for effective teaching and learning. New Directions for Adult and Continuing Education, (50), 41-50.

time machine

WHAT IS IT?

An ice-breaker is an exercise that is used at the beginning of a design project or workshop to help to stimulate constructive interaction. It helps everyone to engage in the dialogue and contribute effectively,

WHY USE THIS METHOD?

1. Helps create a comfortable and productive environment.
2. Helps people get to know each other.
3. Helps participants engage the group and tasks.
4. Helps participants contribute effectively.
5. Creates a sense of community.

CHALLENGES

1. Be aware of time constraints.
2. Should limit the time to 15 to 30 minutes
3. Make it simple
4. It should be fun
5. You should be creative
6. Be enthusiastic
7. If something isn't working move on.
8. Consider your audience
9. Keep in mind technology requirements such as a microphone or projector.
10. Chairs can be arranged in a circle to help participants read body language.
11. Select exercises appropriate for your group.

WHEN TO USE THIS METHOD

1. Define intent

HOW TO USE THIS METHOD

1. The moderator asks each participant to describe where and when they would go if they had a time machine that could travel into the future or the past and to anywhere in the world.

RESOURCES

1. White board
2. Dry erase markers
3. A large comfortable space

REFERENCES

1. Fergueson, S., & Aimone, L. (2002). Making people feel valued. Communication: Journalism Education Today, 36(1), 5-11
2. Sisco, B. R. (1991). Setting the climate for effective teaching and learning. New Directions for Adult and Continuing Education, (50), 41-50.

Chapter 3

Defining the vision

what are we looking for?

3p analysis

WHAT IS IT?
3p analysis is a simple way of analyzing potential decisions to define their value.

The 3 Ps are:
1. Purpose
2. Process
3. Payoff

WHO INVENTED IT?
Ava S, Butler 1996

WHY USE THIS METHOD?
1. Use for planning an agenda for a meeting or for presentations

CHALLENGES
1. Can be subjective

WHEN TO USE THIS METHOD
1. Define intent
2. Make Plans

HOW TO USE THIS METHOD
1. Ask these three questions:
   - What is the purpose?
   - What is the process we will use?
   - What is the anticipated payoff?

RESOURCES
1. Paper
2. Pens
3. Whiteboard
4. Dry erase markers

REFERENCES
1. Butler, Ava S. (1996) Teamthink Publisher: Mcgraw Hill ISBN 0070094330

7p's

WHAT IS IT?

The seven Ps are the product, price, promotion, place, process, physical evidence and people that make up the marketing mix.

WHO INVENTED IT?

Booms and Bitner 1981

WHY USE THIS METHOD?

1. To monitor and respond to change in a positive way.

WHEN TO USE THIS METHOD

1. Define intent
2. Know Context
3. Know User
4. Frame insights

HOW TO USE THIS METHOD

1. The seven p's change rapidly.
2. A successful business must have structures to monitor the seven p's and respond when needed strategically.

RESOURCES

1. Pen
2. Paper
3. White board
4. Dry erase markers
5. Post-it notes

REFERENCES

1. Rajshekhar, G. Javalgi, D. Cutler Bob, and A. Winans William. "At Your Service! does Country of Origin Research Apply to Services?" The Journal of Services Marketing 15.6 (2001): 565–82. ProQuest Research Library. Web. 5 Nov. 20

ACTION PLAN

ACTION PLAN:						
OBJECTIVE:						
No.	ITEM	PERSON	RESOURCE	DATE	ACTUAL	STATUS
1						
2						
3						
4						
5						
6						
7						
8						
9						
10						
11						
12						
13						

action plan

WHAT IS IT?

An action plan is a document that summarizes action items, due dates and other related information.

WHY USE THIS METHOD?

1. To focus team effort.
2. To monitor progress towards a goal.

CHALLENGES

1. Start with the final delivery date required and work backwards to assign delivery dates for individual actions.
2. The action plan should be displayed where it can be accessed by all team members.

WHEN TO USE THIS METHOD

1. Define intent

HOW TO USE THIS METHOD

1. Team brainstorms actions needed to reach a goal and the times when each action should be completed.
2. The moderator draws the action plan on a white board.
3. Team members are assigned responsibility for individual actions.
4. The plan is reviewed by the team to ensure that there are no conflicts.
5. The plan is signed off on by the team.
6. The plan is posted in the project room for future reference.

appreciative inquiry

WHAT IS IT?

Appreciative Inquiry is an organizational method which focuses on developing organization does well. It involves an inquiry which uncovers and appreciates the positive aspects all levels of an organization including customers and suppliers.

WHO INVENTED IT?

Geoffrey Vickers 1968
Stowell and West,1991
West, 1992;
West and Thomas, 2005;
West and Braganca, 2011

WHEN TO USE THIS METHOD

1. Define intent

WHY USE THIS METHOD?

1. Applicable to organizations facing rapid change or growth
2. Appreciating, valuing the Best of What Is
3. Envisioning what might be
4. Engaging in dialogue about what should be
5. Innovating, what will be
6. Build a common vision.
7. Uncover and amplify the positive factors in organizations.
8. Create openness and positive communication between individuals and groups where a negative work environment exists
9. Provide an alternative approach to team building.
10. Show the power and value of teamwork.
11. Illuminating the core values, and practices that support successful teams.
12. Develop communities.

HOW TO USE THIS METHOD

There are a number of approaches to implementing appreciative Inquiry. These include mass interviews and a large, gathering called an appreciative inquiry Summit.

Appreciative inquiry is usually worked out by using a 4-D Cycle

1. "Discovery: People talk to one another, often via structured interviews, to discover the times when their organization is at its best. These stories are told as richly as possible.
2. Dream: The dream phase is commonly run as a large group conference with the help of facilitators. People are encouraged to envision the organization as though the peak moments identified in the discovery phase were the norm rather than the exception.
3. Design: A team is empowered to go away and design ways to create the organization dreamed in the large group conference.
4. Delivery: The final phase delivers the dream and the new design. It is one of experimentation and improvisation. Teams are formed to follow up on the design elements and to continue the appreciative process. This phase may itself contain more small-scale appreciative inquiries into specific aspects of organizational life."

Source: Asian Development Bank

SAMPLE QUESTIONNAIRE?

1. "Think of a peak experience or high point in your work or experience in your organization.
2. In that experience, think about the things you valued most about yourself, the nature of your work, and your organization itself.
3. Think about the core factors that give life to your organization, The really positive values it can build upon.
4. What three wishes would you like to have that would heighten the vitality and health of your organization?"

Source: Asian Development Bank

REFERENCES

1. David Cooperrider, Diana Whitney, and Jacqueline Stavros. 2007. Appreciative Inquiry Handbook. San Francisco: Berrett-Koehler.
2. Appreciative Inquiry Commons. 2008. Available: http://appreciativeinquiry.case.edu
3. Theodore Kinni, "The Art of Appreciative Inquiry", The Harvard Business School Working Knowledge for Business Leaders Newsletter, September 22, 2003.

assumption surfacing

WHAT IS IT?
This is a method of analyzing your assumptions, considering alternative assumptions and prioritizing solutions.

WHO INVENTED IT?
Richard O. Mason, Ian Mitroff 1981

WHY USE THIS METHOD?
1. The purpose of this method is to analyze assumptions to understand which are most plausible and may have the highest impact.
2. A method for approaching ill-structured or "wicked" problems
3. To compare and to evaluate systematically the assumptions of different people.
4. To examine the relationship between underlying assumption

RESOURCES
1. Pen
2. Paper
3. White board
4. Dry Erase markers

WHEN TO USE THIS METHOD
1. Define intent

HOW TO USE THIS METHOD
1. List the decisions that you have made.
2. For each decision list the assumptions that you made
3. Under each assumption list an alternative counter assumption.
4. Delete from your list choices where it makes little difference whether the original assumption or the counter assumption are correct.
5. Analyze the remaining assumptions on a 2x2 matrix high low impact on one axis and high low plausibility on the other axis.
6. High impact and plausibility assumptions should be given high priority.

REFERENCES
1. Mason, R.O., and Mitroff, I.I., 1981; "Challenging Strategic Planning Assumptions: Theory, Cases and Techniques", NY, Wiley, ISBN 0-471-08219-8

bhag

WHAT IS IT?

BHAG stands for Big Hairy Audacious Goal.
It is a type of goal that is bigger than a usual mission statement.

Some examples of BHAGs are:

1. Google bhag is to make all digital information in the world accessible to people everywhere
2. Nokia bhag is to connect one billion people to the internet. For the first time.

WHO INVENTED IT?

J Collins and J Porras,1996

WHY USE THIS METHOD?

1. Bold visions stimulate bold steps
2. BHAGs encourage you to set your sights high and long term.

WHEN TO USE THIS METHOD

Define intent

RESOURCES

1. Pen
2. Paper
3. White board
4. Dry erase markers

HOW TO USE THIS METHOD

1. It needs to motivate people and get them excited.
2. It shouldn't be in your comfort zone
3. It should take a herculean effort to achieve.
4. It should not be possible to achieve with incremental change.
5. BHAGs have time frames of 10-30 years.
6. The BHAG should be aligned to the organization's core values.

REFERENCES

1. Collins, J and Porras, J. Built to Last: Successful Habits of Visionary Companies. Harper Business; 1 edition (November 2, 2004) ISBN-10: 0060566108 ISBN-13: 978-0060566104

boundary examination

WHAT IS IT?
Boundary examination is a way of refining the definition of a problem.

WHO INVENTED IT?
Edward De bono 1982

WHY USE THIS METHOD?
1. The boundary setting may be part of the problem.
2. The boundary may reflect biases.

RESOURCES
1. Pen
2. Paper
3. White board
4. Dry erase markers

WHEN TO USE THIS METHOD
1. Define intent

HOW TO USE THIS METHOD
1. Define the problem with a written statement.
1. Underline the key words
1. Analyze each key word for underlying assumptions.
2. Consider how the meaning of the problem statement changes as the keywords are replaced by synonyms.
1. Redefine the problem boundary by substituting new keywords.

REFERENCES
1. Learn-To-Think: Coursebook and Instructors Manual with Michael Hewitt-Gleeson de Saint-Arnaud (1982), ISBN 0-88496-199-0
2. De Bono's Course in Thinking (1982)

BOWMAN'S STRATEGY CLOCK

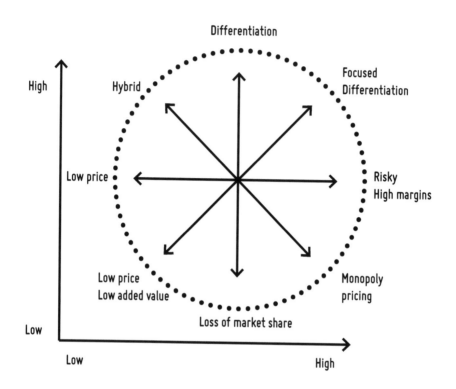

bowman's strategy clock

WHAT IS IT?

This is a method for analyzing the possibility of success for a number of different strategies. It identifies the cost and perceived value of different approaches. Bowman's Strategy Clock has eight alternative strategies in four quadrants.

WHO INVENTED IT?

Cliff Bowman and David Faulkner 1996

WHY USE THIS METHOD?

1. Helps develop a strategy of competitive advantage.
2. Can be used to analyze current strategy and strategies of competitors.

RESOURCES

1. Pen
2. Paper
3. White board
4. Dry erase markers

WHEN TO USE THIS METHOD

1. Define intent

HOW TO USE THIS METHOD

1. Graph competing options on a two axis chart
2. The x axis is high low price
3. The y axis is high low perceived value to the consumer
4. The 8 types of strategy are
- Low price low value
- Low price
- Moderate price and differentiation
- Differentiation
- Focused differentiation
- Increased price and standard product
- High price low value
- Low value and standard price.
- Some of these alternatives are not viable strategies in a competitive environment.

REFERENCES

1. Bowman, C. and Faulkner, D. (1997), "Competitive and Corporate Strategy", Irwin, London.

checklist: environmentally responsible design

Some of the ways in which we can work to improve the environmental performance of the products that we design:

1. Use environmentally responsible strategies appropriate to the product;
2. Reduce overall material content and increase the percentage of recycled material in products;
3. Reduce energy consumption of products that use energy;
4. Specify sustainability grown materials when using wood or agricultural materials;
5. Design disposable products or products that wear out to be more durable and precious;
6. Eliminate unused or unnecessary product features;
7. Design continuously transported products for minimal weight;
8. Design for fast, economical disassembly of major components prior to recycling;
9. Design products so that toxic components are easily removed prior to recycling;
10. Perform comprehensive environmental assessment;
11. Consider all of the ecological impacts from all of the components in the products over its entire life cycle, including extraction of materials from nature, conversion of materials into products, product use, disposal or recycling and transport between these phases;
12. Consider all ecological impacts including global warming, acid rain, smog, habitat damage, human toxicity, water pollution, cancer causing potential, ozone layer depletion and resource depletion;
13. Strive to reduce the largest ecological impacts,
14. Conduct life cycle impact assessment to comprehensively identify opportunities for improving ecological performance
15. Encourage new business models and effective communication
16. Support product 'take back' systems that enable product up-grading and material recycling;
17. Lease the product or sell the service of the product to improve long-term performance and end-of-life product collection;
18. Communicate the sound business value of being ecologically responsible to clients and commissioners
19. Discuss market opportunities for meeting basic needs and reducing consumption,

Source: adapted from design-sustainability.com

reality check

WHAT IS IT?

At each milestone in a design development, the design team and important stakeholders such as customers, clients, manufacturers representatives can meet and review the design to see how real the solution is and refine the direction as necessary.

WHY USE THIS METHOD?

1. It keeps the team honest
2. Makes sure that no important factors have been overlooked.
3. Keeps the stakeholders involved.

CHALLENGES

1. A design project can go off course if the design team work in isolation from stakeholders.

WHEN TO USE THIS METHOD

1. Define intent
2. Know Context
3. Know User
4. Frame insights
5. Explore Concepts
6. Make Plans
7. Deliver Offering

HOW TO USE THIS METHOD

At the conclusion of each phase of a design such as idea generation, research, prototyping and testing, production engineering a meeting of stakeholders should be arranged and a reality check made on whether the design is a real solution . This type of checklist can be worked through with the group.

RESOURCES

1. White board
2. Dry erase markers

REVIEW CHECKLIST QUESTIONS

1. Does the design conform to the design intent statement?
2. Is the design achievable?
3. Have the important risks been identified?
4. Is the design a solution to an identified need or problem?
5. What is the business case for this project?
6. Is the design consistent?
7. Is the design as simple as possible?
8. Are the components recyclable?
9. Can the design be scaled?
10. Are all features necessary?
11. Is everything documented?
12. What are the risks associated with this design?
13. Are any new risks posed by the design that have not been identified?
14. Are the interfaces identified
15. Is the design consistent with the context?
16. Have critical features and interactions been prototyped and tested?
17. Is the cost of ownership reduced?
18. Is the design easy to maintain?
19. Have all legal requirements and regulations been addressed?
20. Have the key stakeholders been identified and involved?
21. What were the assumptions?
22. Is the design usable and accessible?
23. How will the design be implemented?
24. What is the scope of the design?
25. What design alternatives were considered?

briefing checklist: product design

GENERAL
1. What are your contact details?
2. Why is this product being developed?
3. What specific outcomes do we want to achieve?
4. What standards does the product need to conform to?
5. How will the product be used?
6. What is the positioning strategy?
7. What national and international standards does the product need to comply with?
8. Who will approve payment of the invoices?
9. What is your budget?
10. Who will approve the work?

MARKET
1. Who are the intended users?
2. Age gender, culture, location?
3. Who are your competitors?
4. Have you done an intellectual property search?
5. What is your brand?
6. What is your pricing strategy?

MANUFACTURING
1. Who will manufacture the product?
2. What are the preferred materials?
3. What are the preferred manufacturing processes?
4. What is the anticipated release date
5. Will it be released at a particular show or event?
6. What are the anticipated annual manufacturing quantities
7. What batch quantities will it be manufactured in?
8. What is the preferred location of manufacturing?
9. Do you have preferred manufacturing vendors?

DISTRIBUTION
1. What are the preferred distribution channels?
2. How should the product be packaged?
3. Who will maintain the product?
4. How will the product be transported?
5. How will the product be stored?
6. Where will the product be distributed?
7. Are there any other considerations?

briefing checklist: web design

GENERAL
1. What are your objectives?
2. What specific outcomes do we want to achieve?
3. What deliverables do you want?
4. What does your company do?
5. When was your company established?
6. How many employees does your company have?
7. What is your target market or market niche?
8. Who will approve payment of the invoices?
9. What is your budget?
10. Who will approve the work?
11. What is your schedule for the project?

MARKET
1. How do you generate sales
2. How do you generate inquiries
3. How do you obtain information about your customers?
4. What is the age range of your customers?
5. What is the gender breakdown of your customers
6. What occupations do your customers have?
7. Where are your customers located?
8. What languages do your customers speak?
9. Who are your competitors?
10. Can you provide examples of your current marketing materials?
11. Are there examples of web sites that you like or dislike? What are the:
   - Color
   - Images
   - Typography
   - Atmosphere

clarkson ethics principles

WHAT IS IT?

These are a number of principles relating to corporate ethics.

WHO INVENTED IT?

Centre for Corporate Social Performance and Ethics between 1993 and 1998.

WHY USE THIS METHOD?

1. They were a response to corporate scandals connected with management ethics between 2001 and 2003.

WHEN TO USE THIS METHOD

1. Define intent

HOW TO USE THIS METHOD

1. Managers should acknowledge and actively monitor the concerns of all legitimate stakeholders, and should take their interests appropriately into account in decision-making and operations.
2. Managers should listen to and openly communicate with stakeholders about their respective concerns and contributions, and about the risks that they assume because oft heir involvement with the corporation.
3. Managers should adopt processes and modes of behavior that are sensitive to the concerns and capabilities of each stakeholder constituency.
4. Managers should recognize the interdependence of efforts and rewards among stakeholders, and should attempt to achieve a fair distribution of the benefits and burdens of corporate activity among them, taking into account their respective risks and vulnerabilities.
5. Managers should work cooperatively with other entities, both public and private, to insure that risks and harms arising from corporate activities are minimized and, where they cannot be avoided, appropriately compensated.
6. Managers should avoid altogether activities that might jeopardize inalienable human rights or give rise to risks which, if clearly understood, would be patently unacceptable to relevant stakeholders.
7. Managers should acknowledge the potential conflicts between

(a) their own role as corporate stakeholders, and

(b) their legal and moral responsibilities for the interests of stakeholders, and should address such conflicts through open communication, appropriate reporting and incentive systems and, where necessary, third party review.

Source: The Clarkson Principles, http://www.valuebasedmanagement.net/methods_clarkson_principles.html (accessed December 28, 2012).

REFERENCES

1. Joseph W. Weiss – Business Ethics: A Stakeholder and Issues Management Approach.
2. Jeffrey L. Seglin – The Right Thing: Conscience, Profit and Personal Responsibility in Today's Business

Image Copyright Brandon Bourdages, 2012
Used under license from Shutterstock.com

CRITICAL SUCCESS FACTOR CHART

FACTOR   BRAND

	A			B			C			D		
	−	+	++	−	+	++	−	+	++	−	+	++
Cost		x			x				x	x		
Brand			x			x	x					x
Technology		x		x				x		x		
Employees	x				x		x				x	
Customer service		x				x			x		x	
Distribution			x	x				x		x		
Speed to market			x			x	x					x
Design		x		x			x				x	
Reliability		x			x				x			x

critical success factor

WHAT IS IT?
The critical success factor is the factor that is necessary for a project to achieve it's goal or mission. In order to be profitable and survive, a company needs to have a critical success factor.

WHO INVENTED IT?
The term success factor was developed by D. Ronald Daniel of McKinsey & Company in 1961. John F. Rockart further developed the concept of critical success factors between 1979 and 1981

WHY USE THIS METHOD?
1. It is a method of graphically representing a company's critical success factors so they can be the focus for discussion and refinement.
2. It is a method of comparing competitors

CHALLENGES
1. The method can be subjective

RESOURCES
1. Pen
2. Paper
3. Computer
4. Graphics software

WHEN TO USE THIS METHOD
1. Define intent

HOW TO USE THIS METHOD
1. Ask your team: 'Why would customers choose us?'."What do we need to do well to win business?" The answer is typically a critical success factor.
2. Create a matrix and rate each identified critical success factor an a 3 point scale.
3. Graph each score and connect the scores for each company being assessed with a line.

REFERENCES
1. Boynlon, A.C., and Zmud, R.W. 1984. "An Assessment of Critical Success Factors," Sloan Management Review (25:4), pp. 17-27.
2. Rockart, John F. "A Primer on Critical Success Factors" published in The Rise of Managerial Computing: The Best of the Center for Information Systems Research, edited with Christine V. Bullen. (Homewood, IL: Dow Jones-Irwin), 1981, OR, McGraw-Hill School Education Group (1986)
3. Johnson, James A. and Michael Friesen (1995). The Success Paradigm: Creating Organizational Effectiveness Through Quality and Strategy New York: Quorum Books. ISBN 978-0-89930-836-4

DECISION RINGS

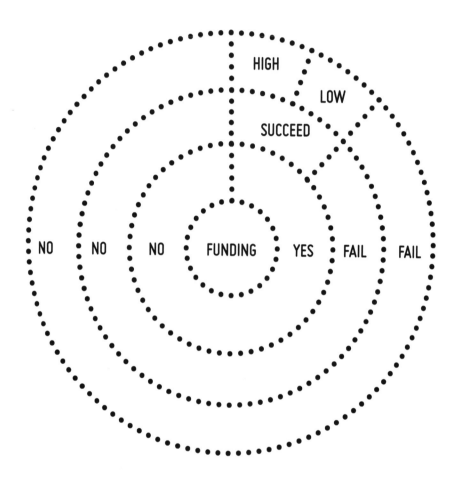

decision rings

WHAT IS IT?

Decision rings are a graphical way of visualizing the likelihood or benefit of the outcome of decisions.

WHY USE THIS METHOD?

1. A visual way of representing a problem.

RESOURCES

1. Pen
2. Paper
3. Computer
4. Software

REFERENCES

1. Tufte, E. (1992), The Visual Display of Quantitative Information, Graphics Press.
2. Baron, J. & R. Brown (1991), Teaching Decisionmaking to Adolescents, Erlbaum.

WHEN TO USE THIS METHOD

1. Define intent
2. Frame insights
3. Explore Concepts
4. Make Plans

HOW TO USE THIS METHOD

1. Draw a number of concentric circles.
2. If your problem decision involves n stages, draw n+1 concentric circles.
3. Split the first ring into segments equal to the number of choices for the first decision.
4. Divide the next stage into segments based on the segments of the previous stage
5. Divide each subsequent segment into the number of boxes equal to the alternative solutions.
6. Divide each subsequent box into boxes proportional to the probability of the associated outcome
7. Repeat for each decision stage.

dialectical inquiry

WHAT IS IT?

Dialectical inquiry is an approach to resolving disagreement that has been central to Indian and European philosophy since ancient times

WHO INVENTED IT?

I Ching 1000BC
Lao Tzu 500BC
Heraclites, Plato, Socrates, Aristoteles, Kant, Hegel, Fichte, Marx, Engels.

WHY USE THIS METHOD?

1. Use for resolution of disagreement through rational discussion, and the search for truth.

De Wit and Meyer mention the following advantages:

1. A range of ideas can be exploited
2. Help focus on points of contention
3. Helps bridge seemingly irreconcilable opposites
4. Finds a synthesis that is better than the trade-off between the opposites.

WHEN TO USE THIS METHOD

1. Define intent
2. Know Context
3. Know User
4. Frame insights
5. Explore Concepts
6. Make Plans
7. Deliver Offering

Image Copyright Dimitrios, 2012
Used under license from Shutterstock.com

HOW TO USE THIS METHOD

Fichtean Dialectics is based upon four concepts:

1. Everything is transient and finite,and exists in time.
2. Everything is composed of opposing contradictions
3. Gradual changes lead to one force overcoming its opponent force
4. Change is helical (spiral), not circular (negation of the negation).

Socratic method is to show that a given hypothesis creates a contradiction; thus, does not represent the truth.

Hegelian dialectic, comprising three dialectical stages of development: a thesis, giving rise to its reaction, an antithesis, which contradicts or negates the thesis, and the tension between the two being resolved by means of a synthesis.

REFERENCES

1. Adler, Mortimer Jerome (2000). "Dialectic". Routledge. Page 4. ISBN 0-415-22550-7
2. Pinto, R. C. (2001). Argument, inference and dialectic: collected papers on informal logic. Argumentation library, vol. 4. Dordrecht:Kluwer Academic. pp. 138–139.

FORCE FIELD DIAGRAM

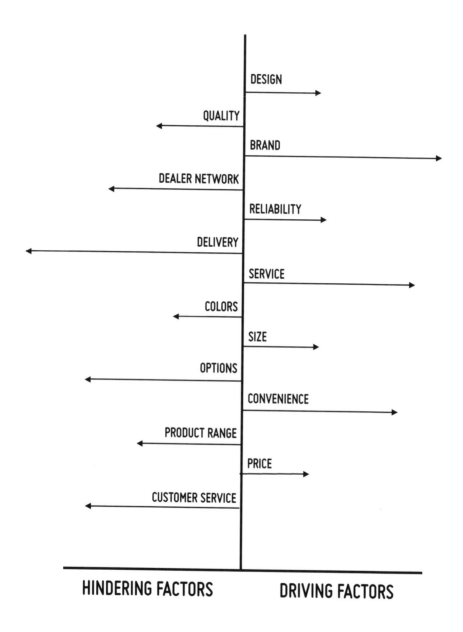

HINDERING FACTORS DRIVING FACTORS

force field analysis

WHAT IS IT?
Force field analysis is a method of mapping and analyzing factors which assist or work against desired goals.

WHO INVENTED IT?
Kurt Lewin 1940s
John R. P. French 1947

WHY USE THIS METHOD?
1. Allows visual comparison of factors affecting the success of a project for discussion of solutions.

CHALLENGES
1. It is best to focus on barriers.
2. Assign a strategy to each barrier

RESOURCES
1. Pen
2. Paper
3. White board
4. Dry erase markers
5. Post-it notes.

REFERENCES
1. Cartwright, D. (1951). Foreword to the 1951 Edition. Field Theory in Social Science and Selected Theoretical Papers–Kurt Lewin. Washington, D.C.: American Psychological Association, 1997. Originally published by Harper & Row.

WHEN TO USE THIS METHOD
1. Define intent
2. Know Context
3. Know User

HOW TO USE THIS METHOD
1. Select a moderator and a team of stakeholders.
2. The moderator describes the problem being focused on to the team
3. The moderator draws the letter T on a white board
4. The moderator writes the problem above the cross stroke on the T
5. The team brainstorms a list of forces working against the goal and the moderator lists them on the right hand of the upstroke on the letter T.
6. The team brainstorms a list or forces working towards the goal and the moderator writes them on the right hand of the upstroke on the letter T.
7. Forces listed can be internal and external.
8. They can be associated with the environment, the organization, people strategy, culture, values, competitors, conflicts or other factors.
9. Prioritize and quantify both lists of forces
10. The moderator draws a horizontal letter T and above the horizontal line draws arrows for each factor indicating their relative significance in the opinion of the team.
11. The moderator draws arrows for each negative factor below the line showing their relative significance.

FUTURE WHEEL

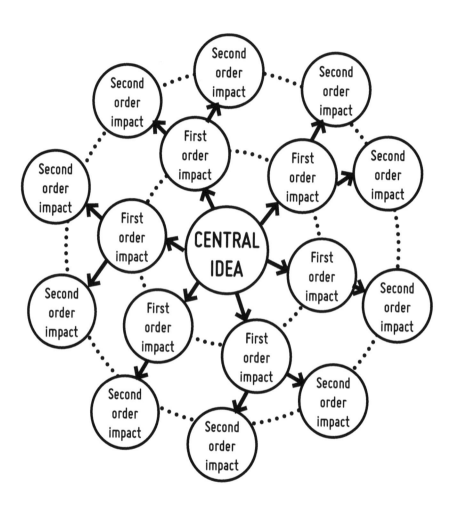

future wheel

WHAT IS IT?
The future wheel is a method to graphically represent and analyze the direct and indirect outcomes of a proposed change.

WHO INVENTED IT?
Jerome Glenn 1972

WHY USE THIS METHOD?
1. A method of envisioning outcomes of decisions.
2. Can be used to study possible outcomes of trends.
3. Helps create a consciousness of the future.

CHALLENGES
1. Can be subjective

WHEN TO USE THIS METHOD
1. Define intent

HOW TO USE THIS METHOD
1. Define the proposed change
2. Identify and graph the first level of outcomes
3. Identify and graph the subsequent level of outcomes
4. Link the dependencies
5. Identify insights
6. Identify the actions
7. Implement the actions

RESOURCES
1. Pen
2. Paper
3. White board
4. Dry erase markers

REFERENCES
1. Futures Wheel, Futures Research Methodology Version 3.0, The Millennium Project, Washington, DC 2009

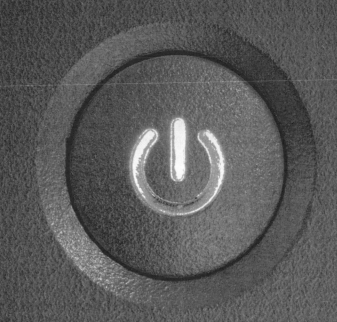

go and no go

WHAT IS IT?
A method to determine when your team is ready to move on to the next discussion item in a meeting.

WHO INVENTED IT?
Ava S, Butler 1996

WHY USE THIS METHOD?
1. Unstructured meetings waste time by trying to discuss all aspects of an issue at once.
2. This method saves time and improves the outcomes and efficiency of meetings.
3. Useful when discussing complex issues

RESOURCES
1. Paper
2. Pens
3. Whiteboard
4. Dry erase markers

WHEN TO USE THIS METHOD
1. Define intent
2. Make Plans

HOW TO USE THIS METHOD
1. When the moderator thinks that it is time to move on to the next agenda item ask:
   ◦ "All in favor of moving on to the next agenda item say Go"
   ◦ "All in favor of not moving forward say No Go"
2. If there are more no go votes the moderator asks "what needs to happen before we will feel comfortable moving forward?"
3. Iterate if necessary.

REFERENCES
1. Butler, Ava S. (1996) Teamthink Publisher: Mcgraw Hill ISBN 0070094330

GOAL GRID

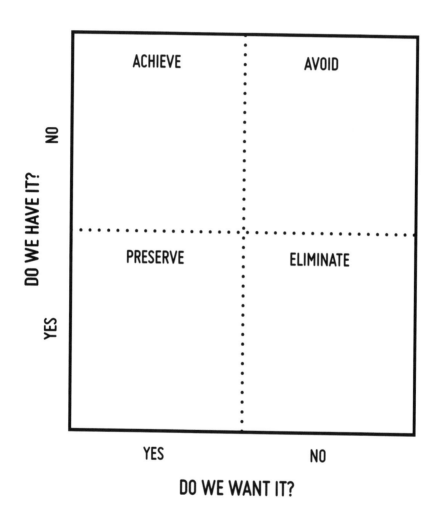

goal grid

WHAT IS IT?

A goal grid is a method for clarifying goals.

"The Goals Grid also provides a structure for analyzing patterns in goals and objectives and for detecting potential conflict with the goals and objectives of others." *Fred Nickols*

WHO INVENTED IT?

Ray Forbes, John Arnold and Fred Nickols 1992

WHY USE THIS METHOD?

1. A goal grid is a method for clarifying goals.

RESOURCES

1. Pen
2. Paper
3. White board
4. Dry erase markers
5. Post-it notes.

WHEN TO USE THIS METHOD

1. Define intent

HOW TO USE THIS METHOD

1. The team brainstorms a list of goals.
2. The moderator asks the team these questions:
   - "Do we have it?"
   - "Do we want it?"
   - "What are we trying to achieve?"
   - "What are we trying to preserve?"
   - "What are we trying to avoid?"
   - "What are we trying to eliminate?"

REFERENCES

1. Arnold, John D. (1980). The Art of Decision Making. AMACOM, New York.
2. Barnard, Chester A (1938). The Functions of the Executive. Harvard University Press, Cambridge
3. Nickols, Fred (2003) The Goals Grid: A Tool for Clarifying Goals & Objectives

goal orientation

WHAT IS IT?

Goal orientation, is a checklist of problem, needs and constraints statements.

WHY USE THIS METHOD?

1. This method helps clarify the intent of the design project.
2. "Learning strategies and self-efficacy are the most important consequences of goal orientation followed by feedback seeking, and organizational outcomes."

Source Payne

HOW TO USE THIS METHOD

1. Write a detailed description of the design problem.
2. Define a list of needs that are connected to the design problem.
3. Make a list of obstacles that need to be overcome to solve the design problem.
4. Make a list of constraints that apply to the problem.
5. Rewrite the problem statement to articulate the above requirements.

WHO INVENTED IT?

J.A. Eison 1970s

WHEN TO USE THIS METHOD

1. Define intent

RESOURCES

1. Pen
2. Paper
3. White board
4. Dry erase markers

REFERENCES

1. DeGeest, D., & Brown, K. G. (2011). The role of goal orientation in leadership development. Human Resource Development Quarterly, 22(2), 157-175.
2. Button, S. B., Mathieu, J. E., & Zajac, D. M. (1996, July). Goal orientation in organizational research: A conceptual and empirical foundation. Organizational Behavior and Human Decision Processes, 67(1), 26-48.

HEPTALYSIS

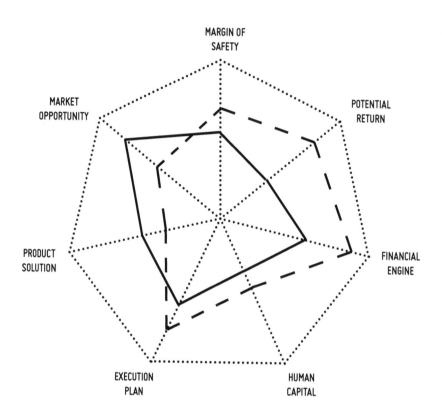

heptalysis

WHAT IS IT?

Heptalysis is a method used to perform an in-depth analysis of early stage businesses ventures using seven criteria for evaluation.

The criteria are:

1. Margin of safety
2. Potential return
3. Financial engine
4. Human capital
5. Execution plan
6. Product solution
7. Market opportunity

WHY USE THIS METHOD?

1. Used for analyzing a new product idea for raising venture capital
2. Use for analyzing what resources are necessary
3. Use for understanding risk.

WHEN TO USE THIS METHOD

1. Define intent
2. Know Context
3. Know User

RESOURCES

1. Pen
2. Paper
3. White board
4. Dry erase markers
5. Post-it notes

HOW TO USE THIS METHOD

Market Opportunity.

1. Who are the potential customers for this product?
2. What is the benefit of it for the customers?
3. Where and how it can be used?
4. What is our advantage over the competitors who produce the same product?
5. Is there a sustainable market for the product?
6. When is the best time to introduce the product to the market

Source Finance NZ, http://financenz.wordpress. com/ (accessed December 28, 2012).

Product/Solution.

1. What are we going to bring to market, service, product or a combination of them?
2. Are there any follow-up products?
3. Are the follow-up products in the scope of our activity?

Execution Plan.

1. Marketing and Promotion
2. Sales and Distribution
3. Production and Quality
4. Compensation
5. Growth
6. Potential Return.
7. What is the expected share of market?
8. What is the pricing strategy?
9. Is the price affordable by the majority of potential customers?
10. How long does it take to achieve profits?

Source: Deepan Siddhu

IS IS NOT CHART

IS – is in scope of this project	IS NOT – is out of scope of this project

is is not

WHAT IS IT?

A method used to define the scope of a project and to create a statement of intent at the start of a project defining the project boundaries.

WHO INVENTED IT?

Tom Kendrick

WHY USE THIS METHOD?

1. This method shows what is inside and outside the scope of a design project.
2. Helps decide what is not going to be considered at this time.

RESOURCES

1. Whiteboard
2. Dry erase markers

REFERENCES

1. Tom Kendrick – Identifying and Managing Project Risk: Essential Tools for Failure-Proofing Your Project AMACOM 2009 ISBN: 0814413404

WHEN TO USE THIS METHOD

1. Define intent

HOW TO USE THIS METHOD

1. Select a moderator.
2. On a white board the moderator creates two headings for two lists "Is" and "Is not."
3. The moderator asks a number of questions
    - When does the problem happen?
    - Where does the problem happen?
    - What is the problem?
    - Who are the stakeholders?
    - Why is there a problem?
    - How does the problem happen?
4. The moderator and team reviews the answers and decide whether each answer belongs in the Is or Is not list.

kaizen method

WHAT IS IT?

Kaizen is a Japanese philosophy for continual incremental change and improvement. It has influenced many management approaches including total quality control. Kaizen focuses on quality, involvement of all, and openness to change.

WHO INVENTED IT?

Masaaki Imai made the term widely known in his book Kaizen: The Key to Japan's competitive success. The Toyota Production System is known for kaizen.

WHY USE THIS METHOD?

1. Helps an organization eliminate waste in business processes
2. Humanizes the workplace
3. Eliminates unnecessary work.
4. Can contribute to large improvements in productivity over time.

CHALLENGES

1. Successful implementation needs the participation of all employees.

WHEN TO USE THIS METHOD

1. Define intent
2. Know Context
3. Know User
4. Frame insights
5. Explore Concepts
6. Make Plans
7. Deliver Offering

HOW TO USE THIS METHOD

The Kaizen approach has 5 elements.

1. Teamwork,
2. Personal discipline,
3. Improved morale,
4. Quality circles,
5. Suggestions for improvement.

REFERENCES

1. Maurer, Robert (2004). One Small Step Can Change Your Life: The Kaizen Way. Workman. ISBN 978-0-7611-2923-3.
2. Liker, Jeffrey; Meier, David (2006). The Toyota Way Fieldbook. New York: McGraw-Hill.
3. Laraia, Anthony C.; Patricia E. Moody, Robert W. Hall (1999). The Kaizen Blitz: accelerating breakthroughs in productivity and performance. John Wiley and Sons. p. 26. ISBN 978-0-471-24648-0.
4. Europe Japan Centre, Kaizen Strategies for Improving Team Performance, Ed. Michael Colenso, London: Pearson Education Limited, 2000

reframing the problem

WHAT IS IT?

This method helps develop innovative solutions with a number of questions.

WHO INVENTED IT?

Tudor Rickards 1974 Manchester Business School

WHY USE THIS METHOD?

1. To create different perspectives and new ideas.

RESOURCES

1. Pen
2. Paper
3. White board
4. Dry Erase markers

REFERENCES

1. Rickards, Tudor (1974). Problem Solving Through Creativity. Wiley. pp. 198. ISBN 0-470-72045-X.
2. Rickards, Tudor; Runco, Mark A., Moger, Susan (2008). 978-0-415-77317-1 The Routledge Companion To Creativity. Routledge. pp. 400. ISBN 978-0-415-77317-1.

WHEN TO USE THIS METHOD

1. Define intent

HOW TO USE THIS METHOD

1. Define the problem that you would like to address.

Complete these sentences while considering your problem.

1. There is more than one way of looking at a problem. You could also define this problem in another way as."
2. "The underlying reason for the problem is."
3. "I think that the best solution is."
4. "If I could break all laws of reality I would try to solve it by."
5. "You could compare this problem to the problem of."
6. "Another, different way of thinking about it is"

kepner tregoe analysis

WHAT IS IT?

Kepner Tregoe analysis is a method for solving problems and making decisions It identifies five stages of analyzing a problem: defining, describing, establishing possible causes, testing the most probable cause and verifying the true cause. It is a method for solving problems, making decisions, and analyzing potential risks and opportunities.

WHO INVENTED IT?

Dr. Charles Kepner and Dr. Benjamin Tregoe 1960s

WHY USE THIS METHOD?

1. Systematic approach
2. Useful when considering many options.
3. Widely respected method in business.
4. Proposes outcome and how to achieve outcome.

CHALLENGES

1. Can be subjective.
2. May be time consuming.

RESOURCES

1. Pen
2. Paper
3. White board
4. Dry erase markers
5. Post-it notes

WHEN TO USE THIS METHOD

1. Frame insights
2. Explore Concepts

HOW TO USE THIS METHOD

1. Prepare a decision statement having the desired result and action required
2. Establish strategic requirements What you must have,
3. Establish your objectives. What you would you like to have?
4. Establish Restraints. The limits of your system.
5. Rank objectives .Generate as many alternatives as possible.
6. Score each alternative using a scale of 1 to 10.
7. Calculate weighted score for each alternative
8. Select the top two or three alternatives.
9. List negative consequences for each top alternative
10. Select the preferred alternative.
11. Take action.

REFERENCES

1. Charles H. Kepner and Benjamin B. Tregoe The New Rational Manager
2. Dean L. Gano a.o. – Apollo Root Cause Analysis

key performance indicator

WHAT IS IT?

A Key performance indicator is a method of analyzing the success of an activity. Key performance indicators are used to monitor the success of an organization. They should be understandable, measurable and meaningful.

WHY USE THIS METHOD?

1. Key performance indicators are a performance management tool.
2. Good Key performance indicators give employees and team members a focus for what is most important.

CHALLENGES

1. Key performance indicators must be measurable factors.

RESOURCES

1. Pen
2. Paper
3. Computer
4. Graphics software

WHEN TO USE THIS METHOD

1. Define intent
2. Know Context
3. Frame insights

HOW TO USE THIS METHOD

Set a target for each performance indicators.

1. The key stages in identifying Key performance indicators are:
   ◦ Having a pre-defined business process.
   ◦ Having requirements for the BPs.
   ◦ Having a quantitative/qualitative measurement of the results and comparison with set goals.
   ◦ Make team aware of key performance indicators.
2. Analyze variances and adjust processes and resources to meet key performance indicator goals

REFERENCES

1. Fitz-Gibbon, Carol Taylor (1990), "Performance indicators", BERA Dialogues (2), ISBN 978-1-85359-092-4
2. Parmenter, David (2007) Key Performance Indicators. John Wiley & Sons, ISBN 0-470-09588-1.

kick off meeting

WHAT IS IT?

A kick off meeting is the first meeting of a design project with the project team. In a kick off meeting project roles and responsibilities, objectives and rules, schedule and processes are defined.

WHY USE THIS METHOD?

1. Useful for getting all team members in alignment.
2. Opportunity to energize design team.

CHALLENGES

1. Requires planning

RESOURCES

1. Project space
2. Whiteboard
3. Dry erase markers
4. Notebooks
5. Pens

WHEN TO USE THIS METHOD

1. Define intent

HOW TO USE THIS METHOD

Appoint a project manager

Invite stakeholders

Sample agenda:

1. Introductions of stakeholders
2. Overview and background.
3. Project objectives
4. Project plan and timeline
5. Deliverables
6. Project management process
7. Project space
8. Weekly meetings
9. Reporting
10. Communication plan
11. Change control
12. Contact list
13. Status reports
14. Issues
15. Set expectations
16. Project resources
17. Meeting minutes
18. File location and distribution
19. Project team and their roles
20. Risk management
21. Meeting summary
22. Action items
23. Meeting questions and answers

likert scale

WHAT IS IT?

A Likert Scale is a response scale used in questionnaires which defines a participant's degree of agreement with a statement.

WHO INVENTED IT?

Rensis Likert 1932

WHY USE THIS METHOD?

1. May be easy to analyze
2. Simple to prepare
3. Easy to complete for participants

CHALLENGES

1. Respondents avoid extreme responses
2. Central response bias
3. Participants may agree with statements to please the researchers rather than present their feelings.
4. Participants may seek to present themselves in a more socially acceptable way than they would if they answer the questions based on their feelings.

WHEN TO USE THIS METHOD

1. Know Context
2. Know User
3. Frame insights
4. Explore Concepts

HOW TO USE THIS METHOD

1. Participants are given a series of attitude questions
2. For each question ask whether, they have strong feelings to each using question a point rating scale.
3. The format of a five-level Likert item, is:
   - Strongly disagree
   - Disagree
   - Neither agree nor disagree
   - Agree
   - Strongly agree
4. Total the scores
5. Seven and ten level Likert scales are also sometimes used.

RESOURCES

1. Prepared questionnaires
2. Pens
3. Calculator or computer

REFERENCES

1. Burns, Alvin; Burns, Ronald (2008). Basic Marketing Research (Second ed.). New Jersey: Pearson Education. pp. 250. ISBN 978-0-13-205958-9.
2. Carifio, James and Rocco J. Perla. (2007) Ten Common Misunderstandings, Misconceptions, Persistent Myths and Urban Legends about Likert Scales and Likert Response Formats and their Antidotes. Journal of Social Sciences 3 (3): 106-116

MEETING EVALUATION

Meeting started on time	1	2	3	4	5
Agenda was distributed before the meeting	1	2	3	4	5
The meeting followed the agenda	1	2	3	4	5
All attendees participated	1	2	3	4	5
The meeting was an effective use of time	1	2	3	4	5
Progress was made	1	2	3	4	5
The team reached collective decisions	1	2	3	4	5
The facilitator summarized the results	1	2	3	4	5
Tasks were allocated	1	2	3	4	5
Previous meeting tasks were completed	1	2	3	4	5
The purpose of the meeting was clear	1	2	3	4	5
The meeting finished on time	1	2	3	4	5
TOTAL					

1:Very Unsatisfactory   2:Unsatisfactory   3:Average   4:Satisfactory   5 Very satisfactory

meeting evaluation

WHAT IS IT?

This method is an organized way of monitoring the teams perceptions of the effectiveness and content of team meetings.

WHY USE THIS METHOD?

1. To monitor the effectiveness of team meetings
2. To find areas of possible improvement in team meeting process and procedures.

WHEN TO USE THIS METHOD

1. Define intent
2. Know Context
3. Know User
4. Frame insights
5. Explore Concepts
6. Make Plans
7. Deliver Offering

HOW TO USE THIS METHOD

1. Team members complete the evaluation reports after each meeting or as required.
2. The meeting moderator reviews the evaluations and reports the results to the team at the beginning of the next meeting.
3. The team discusses the results of the previous review.
4. The moderator analyzes trends in evaluations over a number of meetings.

RESOURCES

1. Evaluation forms can be printed or online.

mirror

WHAT IS IT?

This method allows teams to review each other and analyze another teams performance and share information.

WHY USE THIS METHOD?

1. Improves effectiveness of teams
2. Allows sharing of information

WHEN TO USE THIS METHOD

1. Define intent
2. Know Context
3. Know User
4. Frame insights
5. Explore Concepts
6. Make Plans
7. Deliver Offering

HOW TO USE THIS METHOD

1. Moderator presents a number of questions to two teams.
2. Each team moves into a separate private space to discuss the questions.
3. The teams create a list of conclusions
4. Teams return to shared space
5. Teams present their conclusions.
6. Group discussion with moderator where both teams discuss other teams observations and reach agreement on changes to improve team effectiveness.

RESOURCES

1. Two private spaces
2. White boards
3. Dry erase markers
4. Post-it-notes
5. Pens
6. Paper.

87

mission statement

WHAT IS IT?

A mission statement is a summary of purpose of an organization or person and it's primary goal. The mission statement should guide the actions of the organization,

A mission statement should:
1. "Define what the company is
2. Limited to exclude some ventures
3. Broad enough to allow for creative growth
4. Distinguish the company from all others
5. Serve as framework to evaluate current activities
6. Stated clearly so that it is understood by all."

Source Vern McGinis

REFERENCES

1. Haschak, Paul G. (1998). Corporate statements: the official missions, goals, principles and philosophies of over 900 companies. Jefferson, N.C: McFarland. ISBN 0-7864-0342-X.

WHEN TO USE THIS METHOD

1. Define intent

CHALLENGES

1. A good mission statement should not have to be revised every few years.

WHY USE THIS METHOD?

1. A good mission statement provides strategic vision and direction for the organization.

HOW TO USE THIS METHOD

1. List the organization's unique strengths and weaknesses.
2. List the organization's primary stakeholders
3. Interview the stakeholders to understand how they perceive the organization.
4. Write a one-sentence description of each stakeholders strength pairing.
5. Combine any that are similar.
6. Prioritize the sentences in order of importance to the vision.
7. Make one sentence from the high priority sentences
8. Get some customers to review the vision statement and comment.
9. Review the statement in a brainstorming session with your employees.
10. Ask your suppliers to review the statement
11. Refine the statement based on the feedback that you have .
12. When you have refined the paragraph into statements that clearly articulates the way the company wants to relate to those it effects,communicate to stakeholders for feedback and refine.

moscow prioritization

WHAT IS IT?

Moscow is a method of analyzing and prioritizing goals. The four factors of analysis are:

1. Must
2. Should
3. Could
4. Will not

WHO INVENTED IT?

Dai Clegg, Oracle UK

WHY USE THIS METHOD?

1. Useful in planning
2. Useful in negotiations to understand the relative importance of goals.

RESOURCES

1. Pen
2. Paper
3. White board
4. Dry erase markers
5. Post-it notes

WHEN TO USE THIS METHOD

1. Define intent

HOW TO USE THIS METHOD

With your team analyze your organization according to the following criteria. MOSCOW is a checklist for discussion.

1. Must have or else delivery will be a failure
2. Should have otherwise will have to adopt a workaround
3. Could have to increase delivery satisfaction
4. Would like to have in the future but won't have now

Source: [1]

REFERENCES

1. A Guide to the Business Analysis Body of Knowledge. International Institute of Business Analysis. 2009. ISBN 978-0-9811292-1-1.
2. Clegg, Dai; Barker, Richard (2004-11-09). Case Method Fast-Track: A RAD Approach. Addison-Wesley. ISBN 978-0-201-62432-8.

most analysis

WHAT IS IT?

Most analysis is an internal strategic analysis method used to plan the strategy for an organization. MOST stands for:

1. Mission: where you intend the business to go
2. Objectives: the key goals needed to achieve your mission
3. Strategies: the options open to you to achieve your goals
4. Tactics: how to put these strategies into action

WHY USE THIS METHOD?

1. Systematic approach for planning strategy.

WHEN TO USE THIS METHOD

1. Define intent
2. Know Context
3. Know User
4. Frame insights

HOW TO USE THIS METHOD

MOST is a checklist for discussion.

1. Mission: This is the reason for existence of any organization. It is an instruction stating what business the organization is in and what it is intending to achieve.
2. Objectives: These are short term or long term goals set to fulfil the mission set for an organization.
3. Strategy: It is the step by step approach taken to achieve short term and long term goals.

Source: Strategic Analysis and Implementation, PEST Analysis, Porter .., http://ba-resources. co.uk/strategic-analysis-and-implementation. php (accessed December 28, 2012)

RESOURCES

1. Pen
2. Paper
3. White board
4. Dry erase markers
5. Post-it notes

catwoe

WHAT IS IT?

'CATWOE' is a mnemonic applied to the system containing the problem or intent of the design. It is a method used to determine the problem to be addressed by a design.

WHO INVENTED IT?

Prof Gwilym Jenkins University of Lancaster 1966, Peter Checkland 1990

WHY USE THIS METHOD?

1. Can be used to help define a strategy
2. Can be used to help define the core problem to be addressed.

CHALLENGES

1. All aspects should be considered but do not need to be part of the final problem definition.

REFERENCES

1. Checkland and Scholes, Soft Systems Methodology in Action, 1990

WHEN TO USE THIS METHOD

1. Define intent

HOW TO USE THIS METHOD

Analyze your system to identify the core problem to be addressed before starting the design process to ensure that you are considering all aspects of the system. CATWOE is a checklist for discussion

1. Customers – Who are the customers and how will they be affected
2. Actors – Who are the stakeholders and how will it affect them?
3. Transformation Process – What systems are affected?
4. World View – What is the big picture and what are the large scale impacts?
5. Owner – Who owns the design and what role will they play in the solution?
6. Environmental Constraints – What will be the environmental impacts?

RESOURCES

1. Pen
2. Paper
3. White board
4. Dry erase markers
5. Post-it notes

MULTIVOTING SCORE SHEET

A		N	
B		O	
C		P	
D		Q	
E		R	
F		S	
G		T	
H		U	
I		V	
J		W	
K		X	
L		Y	
M		Z	

multivoting

WHAT IS IT?

Multivoting is a method used by a team to reduce a long list of items to a manageable number in order to identify what is most important.

WHY USE THIS METHOD?

1. Reduces a list°
2. Prioritizes a list
3. Identifies important items

CHALLENGES

1. If you have less than 5 people have one or two votes per person. If you have between 6 and 15 people have 3 votes. If you have more than 15, have 4 votes.
2. You can use a secret ballot to vote.

WHEN TO USE THIS METHOD

1. Explore Concepts

HOW TO USE THIS METHOD

1. Work from a large list
2. Assign letter to each item
3. Vote
4. Vote, using a show of hands.
5. Each person votes for one-tenth of the total items. So if there are 100 items, each person has ten votes.
6. Tally the votes
7. Repeat as necessary.
8. Prioritize the concepts based on the number of votes.

RESOURCES

1. Pen
2. Paper
3. White board
4. Dry erase markers

OCTAGON

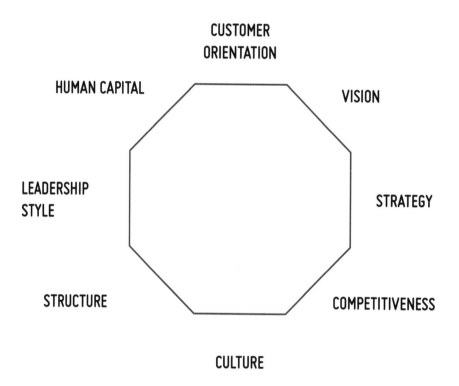

CUSTOMER ORIENTATION

HUMAN CAPITAL

VISION

LEADERSHIP STYLE

STRATEGY

STRUCTURE

COMPETITIVENESS

CULTURE

octagon

WHAT IS IT?

The Octagon is a method that can be used in interviews with organizational stakeholders to help understand the intangible factors of an organization's culture and leadership style.

WHO INVENTED IT?

Bossard Consulting

WHY USE THIS METHOD?

1. To gain an understanding of stakeholders in an organization.

CHALLENGES

1. Obtain authorization to use statements.

WHEN TO USE THIS METHOD

1. Know Context
2. Know User
3. Frame insights

HOW TO USE THIS METHOD

1. Select a group of managers or stakeholders in an organization.
2. Conduct interviews with each stakeholder and ask each to supply a short single sentence comment on each of the Octagon headings.
3. Analyze the statements.
4. Create a list of insights.

RESOURCES

1. Pen
2. Paper
3. Note pad
4. Prepared forms with questions.

OHMAE STRATEGIC TRIANGLE

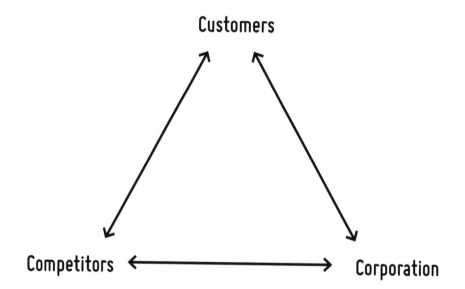

ohmae 3c model

WHAT IS IT?
Ohmae's 3C Model is a strategic planning tool that focuses on three factors needed for business success, customers, competitors and the corporation.

WHO INVENTED IT?
Kenichi Ohmae 1982

WHY USE THIS METHOD?
1. A sustained competitive advantage can only exist by integrating the 3cs

CHALLENGES
1. The organization does not need to lead in every function.

WHEN TO USE THIS METHOD
1. Define intent

HOW TO USE THIS METHOD
1. An organization needs a customer, competitor or corporation based strategy or combination of strategies to be successful.
2. This is not a step-by-step methodology.

RESOURCES
1. Pens
2. Paper
3. White board
4. Dry erase markers
5. Post-it-notes

REFERENCES
1. Ohmae, K. The Mind Of The Strategist: The Art of Japanese Business. 1 Aug 1991 |ISBN-10: 0070479046 ISBN-13: 978-0070479043

pestel analysis

WHAT IS IT?

A PESTEL analysis is an external environmental analysis of an organization. It is a popular method in the United Kingdom. Related methods are PEST, PESTLE, STEEPLE, STEP and ETPS

WHO INVENTED IT?

Francis J. Aguilar 1967,
Fahey, Narayanan, Morrison, Renfro, Boucher, Mecca and Porte 1980s

WHY USE THIS METHOD?

1. Use PESTEL analysis for business and strategic planning, marketing planning, business and product development.

CHALLENGES

1. A PESTEL analysis can be used prior to undertaking a SWOT analysis to better understand opportunities and threats.

WHEN TO USE THIS METHOD

1. Define intent
2. Know Context
3. Know User
4. Frame insights

HOW TO USE THIS METHOD

1. Political Local, national and international
2. Economic Local, national and international.
3. Sociological influences on an organization.
4. Technological influences and trends.
5. Legal factors. Local, national and international
6. Environmental factors. Local, national and international

RESOURCES

1. White board
2. Dry erase markers
3. Camera
4. Paper
5. Pens
6. Post-it-notes

REFERENCES

1. Porter, Michael. "The Five Competitive Forces That Shape Strategy". The Harvard Business Review. Retrieved March 28, 2012.

POLITICAL

1. Current national policy
2. National strategic documents and consultations impacting on you
3. Local commissioning consultations and
4. Strategic Planning Processes
5. Local government structure and annual reports
6. Local healthcare needs

ECONOMIC

1. The budget and pre-budget review
2. Current political view on public finance and business growth
3. Your local authority's spending review process
4. Sources of grant funding and investment
5. Potential new markets and sales opportunities
6. Job growth
7. Tariffs
8. Inflation

SOCIAL

1. Current health and social trends at local and national level
2. Make up and demographics of your local population or marketplace
3. Current media topics
4. Public reaction to recent local events
5. Reach into local marketplace
6. Diversity
7. Trends
8. Health
9. Leisure activities

TECHNOLOGICAL

1. Is your information communication
2. Technology up to date?
3. What systems and processes are prevalent in the market place?
4. If you are in service delivery, what's
5. Considered best practice?
6. Have your staff training and qualifications needs changed?

ENVIRONMENTAL

1. Environmental regulation
2. Reduction of carbon footprint
3. Sustainability
4. Market values
5. Stakeholder and investor values.
6. Environmental issues
   ◦ International
   ◦ National
   ◦ Local
7. Organizational environmental Impact
8. Local impact of adverse weather

LEGAL

1. Employment law
2. Health and safety regulation
3. Equality and diversity law
4. Environmental regulations.
5. Consumer protection laws.
6. Tax compliance
7. Competitive regulations.
8. Regulatory bodies
9. Sector specific regulatory compliance

POLARITIES MATRIX

POLARITIES	++	+	0	–	––
PRICE					
CUSTOMER SERVICE					
QUALITY					
DELIVERY					
DESIGN					
ENVIRONMENTAL SUSTAINABILITY					
SERVICE					
DISTRIBUTION					
OPTIONS					
RELIABILITY					
PERFORMANCE					
BRAND					
INVESTMENT					
VISIBILITY					
SIMPLICITY					

• • • • • • • • • • • • OUR PRODUCT

━━━━━━━━━ COMPETITOR'S PRODUCT

Source: Haberfelner

polarities matrix

WHAT IS IT?
The polarities tool is a method of graphically comparing a number of alternatives.

WHY USE THIS METHOD?
1. It is used when there are a number of sub criteria to compare for a small number of options.
2. This method is used to compare factors related to a number of competitors.

REFERENCES
1. Olivier L. de Weck, Ernst Fricke, Siegfried Vössner Reinhard Haberfellner Orell Fuessli Verlag Systems Engineering (January 1, 2012) ISBN-10: 328004068X ISBN-13: 978-3280040683

WHEN TO USE THIS METHOD
1. Know Context
2. Know User
3. Frame insights

HOW TO USE THIS METHOD
1. Collect the required data.
2. Define a scale
3. Evaluate each criteria
4. Add each item to your graph

RESOURCES
1. Pen
2. Paper
3. Data

POWERGRAM

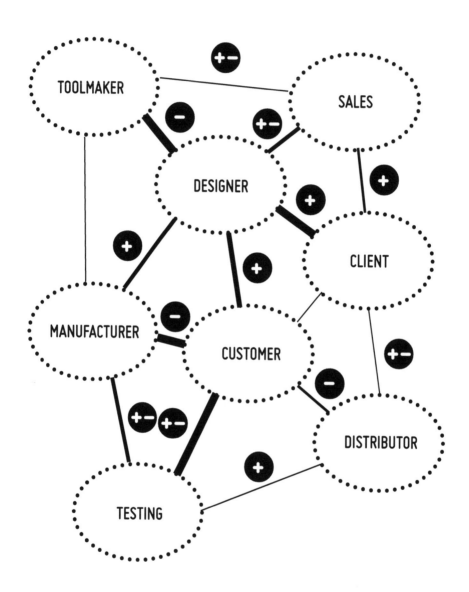

powergram

WHAT IS IT?

"A powergram is a graphical representation of the power dynamics, and power positions, within an account. It shows the true power structure, which is usually different than the account's organizational chart. It provides useful insights about an account's decision making process." *Source: Greg Alexander*

WHO INVENTED IT?

Greg Alexander

WHY USE THIS METHOD?

1. A more descriptive method than an organizational chart.
2. Can illustrate unofficial power structures.
3. Can be used to generate debate and discussion on roles and responsibilities.

CHALLENGES

1. Can be subjective.
2. Rank does not equal power.

WHEN TO USE THIS METHOD

1. Define intent
2. Know Context

HOW TO USE THIS METHOD

1. "Identify the formal lines of reporting and authority.
2. A circle represents a person
3. Identify the stakeholders you like to include
4. The larger the circle, the more power '
5. A line denotes a relationship
6. The heavier the line, the stronger the relationship
7. A strike through a line means a negative relationship
8. A shorter line represents a closer relationship,or frequent contact
9. A longer line represents a more distant the relationship"

Source: Greg Alexander

RESOURCES

1. Pen
2. Paper
3. Post-it-notes
4. White board
5. Dry erase pens

REFERENCES

1. Brill, Peter L. and Richard Worth. The four levers of corporate change. New York : AMACOM, 1997.

premortem

WHAT IS IT?

The premortem is a risk-mitigation planning tool that attempts to identify project threats at the outset.

WHO INVENTED IT?

Gary Klein, 1998

WHY USE THIS METHOD?

1. The Premortem technique is low cost and high value

WHEN TO USE THIS METHOD

1. Define intent

REFERENCES

2. Klein., Gary. Sources of Power: How People Make Decisions. 1998. MIT Press.

RESOURCES

1. Evaluation forms can be printed or online.

HOW TO USE THIS METHOD

1. Determine a period after completion of the project when it should be known whether the project was successful. It could be one or five years.
2. Imagine the project was a complete failure.
3. What could have been the cause?
4. Ask each team member to suggest ten reasons for the failure.
5. Think about the internal and external context and the stakeholders relationships.
6. Ask each team meber to select one of the reasons for failure they have listed and describe it to the group.
7. Each person should present one reason.
8. Collect and review the full list of reasons from each participant.
9. Review the session and strengthen the strategy based on the premortem.

REQUIREMENTS CATALOG

NO.	CATEGORY	DESCRIPTION: ABILITY TO	IMPORTANCE	REF.	FREQ. OF USE
	Core functions				
	Security				
	Financial audit				
	System audit				
	System control				
	System backup				
	Reports,				
	Performance				
	Access				
	Data protection				
	Archiving				

requirements catalog

WHAT IS IT?
A requirements catalog is a list of requirements for the design of a system from a business perspective

WHY USE THIS METHOD?
1. A requirements catalog provides an overview of what a system should do and when it should do it in order to create value for a business.

RESOURCES
1. Pen
2. Paper
3. Computer
4. Spread sheet software

WHEN TO USE THIS METHOD
1. Define intent

HOW TO USE THIS METHOD
1. List the functions of the system,
2. Describe each function's ability.
3. List the frequency of use of each function.
4. Assign a value to indicate the importance to each function.

RISK MAP

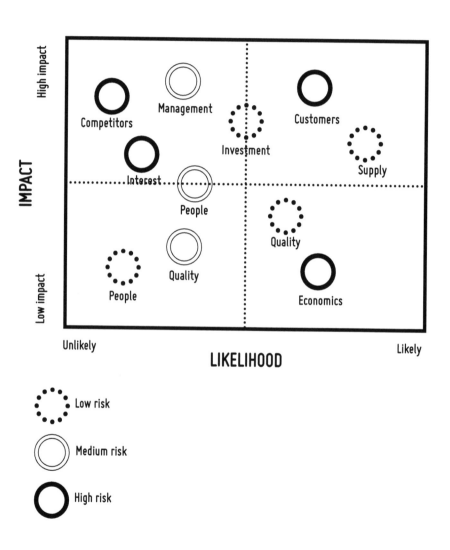

risk map

WHAT IS IT?

A risk map is a method of analyzing risk in order to understand which risks may require action or strategy to control.

WHY USE THIS METHOD?

1. To identify risks
2. To exploit opportunities
3. To control the impact of risks.

RESOURCES

1. Pen
2. Paper
3. White board
4. Dry erase markers
5. Post-it notes

REFERENCES

1. Crockford, Neil (1986). An Introduction to Risk Management (2 ed.). Cambridge, UK: Woodhead-Faulkner. p. 18. ISBN 0-85941-332-2.
2. Flyvbjerg, B., 2006, ""From Nobel Prize to Project Management: Getting Risks Right." Project Management Journal, vol. 37, no. 3, August 2006, pp. 5-15.

WHEN TO USE THIS METHOD

1. Define intent
2. Frame insights
3. Explore Concepts

HOW TO USE THIS METHOD

1. Collect primary research through qualitative and quantitative methods such as focus groups or questionnaires.
2. Collect secondary research data.
3. Analyze data.
4. Create a list of risk issues using the headings: process, people, requirements, schedule, cost, environment, and others.
5. Draw a risk map graphing each by the perception of whether it is controllable or not controllable and observable or not observable.
6. Crete a second map and plot each risk by the likely impact and how likely the risk event is to occur.
7. Identify ways to reduce risks
8. Prioritize risk reduction strategies.
9. Be transparent and inclusive
10. Continually re-assess risk

RISK REWARD ANALYSIS

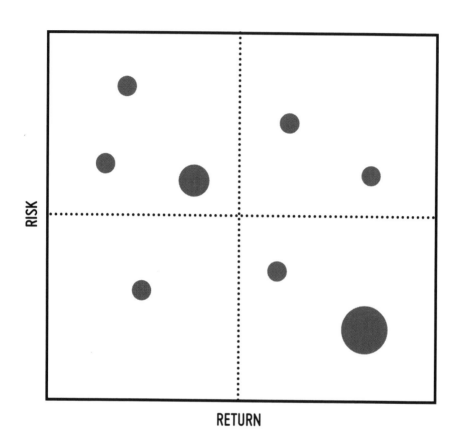

risk reward analysis

WHAT IS IT?

A risk-reward analysis is a method to assess the risk and reward of a number of different ideas.

WHY USE THIS METHOD?

1. For comparing different strategic directions for the company.
2. For deciding which projects to keep within the program and which to discard.
3. Use by an individual team member deciding how best to spend their day.

WHEN TO USE THIS METHOD

1. Define intent
2. Frame insights
3. Explore Concepts
4. Make Plans

HOW TO USE THIS METHOD

1. Create a list of all the different options and their possible rewards.
2. Plot the alternatives on the risk-reward chart.
3. The bigger the bubble the more resources are required to execute that option.
4. Analyze the chart to determine where the best balance of risk and reward is to be found.

RESOURCES

1. Pen
2. Paper
3. White board
4. Dry erase markers
5. Post-it notes

Customer
Manager
Supplier

rotating roles

WHAT IS IT?
Rotating roles is a method of creating different perspectives to help solve problems more effectively and efficiently.

WHY USE THIS METHOD?
1. To create more perspectives relative to a problem.

WHEN TO USE THIS METHOD
2. Know Context
3. Know User
4. Frame insights
5. Explore Concepts

RESOURCES
1. Pen
2. Paper
3. White board
4. Dry erase markers
5. Post-it notes
6. Large table
7. Chairs.

HOW TO USE THIS METHOD
1. Create team of 4 to 8 participants.
2. Designate each chair around a table as a particular role such as manager, customer, supplier, designer, engineer, factory worker.
3. Participants take seats around the table.
4. The moderator asks a number of questions which the participants respond to with insights and ideas from the perspective of the role defined by the seat that they occupy.
5. The moderator or an assistant records responses on a white board. You can video the session.
6. The participants move to the next chair at the end of each round of questions.
7. The moderator summarizes the replies.
8. The team creates a list of insights based on the replies.

REFERENCES
1. Tool Navigator, The Master Guide for Teams by Walter j. Michalski, Productivity Press 1997, USA
2. Business Creativity, Breaking the invisible barriers by Arthur Gogatz and Reuben Mondejar, Palgrave Macmillan 2005, Great Britain
3. McFadzean, E.S. [1998], The Creativity Tool Box: A Practical Guide for Facilitating Creative Problem Solving Sessions, TeamTalk Consulting, Milton Keynes.

WORD LISTS

VERB LIST	ADJECTIVE LIST	ADVERB LIST	PRODUCT LIST
walk	adaptable	accidentally	GPS
stand	adventurous	anxiously	marine
reach	affable	beautifully	printer
sit	affectionate	blindly	copy
jump	agreeable	boldly	chair
fly	ambitious	bravely	sofa
accept	amiable	brightly	video
allow	amicable	calmly	game
advise	amusing	carefully	camera
answer	brave	carelessly	desk
arrive	bright	cautiously	tv
ask	broad-minded	clearly	music
avoid	calm	correctly	floor
stop	careful	courageously	bookcase
agree	charming	cruelly	tools
deliver	communicative	daringly	fence
depend	compassionate	deliberately	cart
describe	conscientious	doubtfully	car
deserve	considerate	eagerly	house
destroy	convivial	easily	bean bag
disappear	courageous	elegantly	audio

semantic intuition

WHAT IS IT?
Semantic intuition is a method of generating ideas based on word associations.

WHO INVENTED IT?
Warfield, Geschka, & Hamilton, 1975. Battelle Institute

WHY USE THIS METHOD?
1. To find new solutions to a problem.

WHEN TO USE THIS METHOD
1. Explore Concepts

RESOURCES
1. Pens
2. Paper
3. Post-it -notes
4. White board
5. Dry erase markers.

HOW TO USE THIS METHOD
1. Define the problem to be explored.
2. The team brainstorms two to four word lists that are related to the problem. They could be for example a list of nouns, a list of verbs and a list of adjectives.
3. The team makes a forth lists of associations of two or three words from the lists that can form the basis of new ideas.
4. Combine one word from one set with another word from the other set.
5. The team visualizes new products services or experiences based on the word associations.
6. Each team member produces five to ten ideas based on the word associations over a 30 minute period.
7. The ideas are prioritized by the group by voting.

REFERENCES
1. Warfield, J. N., H. Geschka, and R. Hamilton, Methods of Idea Management, Approaches to Problem Solving No. 4, Columbus: Academy for Contemporary Problems, August, 1975.

shredded questions

WHAT IS IT?

Shredded questions is a method of creating an orderly process for a team to address an agenda item in a meeting.

WHO INVENTED IT?

Ava S, Butler 1996

WHY USE THIS METHOD?

1. Use for planning an agenda for a meeting or for presentations
1. Unstructured meetings waste time by trying to discuss all aspects of an issue at once.
2. This method saves time and improves the outcomes and efficiency of meetings.
3. Useful when discussing complex issues
4.

CHALLENGES

1. If questions do not work in meeting ask the group to help in refining the questions.

WHEN TO USE THIS METHOD

1. Define intent
2. Make Plans

HOW TO USE THIS METHOD

Before the meeting determine the best questions to guide the discussion. Include questions that will cover the following factors:

1. Facts
2. Feelings
3. Creative alternatives
4. The pros of each alternative
5. The cons of each alternative
6. Agreement on decisions
7. Next steps

RESOURCES

1. Paper
2. Pens
3. Whiteboard
4. Dry erase markers

REFERENCES

1. Butler, Ava S. (1996) Teamthink Publisher: Mcgraw Hill ISBN 0070094330

INTERNAL STAKEHOLDERS

FUNCTION	NAME 1	NAME 2	NAME 3	NAME 4
MARKETING				
SALES				
CUST. SERVICE				
HR				
IT				
ENGINEERING				
DESIGN				
MANAGEMENT				
FINANCE				
EMPLOYEES				
REPS				

Out of scope ☐   In scope ☐   Highest priority ☐

EXTERNAL STAKEHOLDERS

FUNCTION	NAME 1	NAME 2	NAME 3	NAME 4
COMPETITORS				
GOVERNMENT				
CUSTOMERS				
SUPPLIERS				
MEDIA				
CLIENTS				

stakeholder scope map

WHAT IS IT?
A stakeholder scope map is a map that indicates the priority and scope of stakeholders in a project

WHO INVENTED IT?
Mel Silberman 2000

WHY USE THIS METHOD?
1. The map assists in identifying which stakeholders should be given priority during a project.

CHALLENGES
1. Should not be too detailed

REFERENCES
1. The Consultant's Toolkit: High-Impact Questionnaires, Activities and How-to. Guides for Diagnosing and Solving Client Problems, Mel Silberman (2000)

WHEN TO USE THIS METHOD
1. Define intent

HOW TO USE THIS METHOD
1. Brainstorm with your design team a list of internal stakeholders and a list of external stakeholders.
2. Determine which stakeholders are highest priority and which stakeholders are inside and outside the scope of the project management process.
3. Identify conflicts of interest.

RESOURCES
1. Pens
2. Paper
3. White board
4. Dry erase markers
5. Post-it-notes

trajectories of change

WHAT IS IT?

The Four Trajectories of Industry Change is a model why industries change and how they change developed by Anita M. McGahan

WHO INVENTED IT?

Anita M. McGahan 2004

WHY USE THIS METHOD?

1. The goal of this method is to develop more effective strategy for long term change.

CHALLENGES

1. Resisting industry change is often not possible.
2. Organizations should plan to evolve with industry change.

WHEN TO USE THIS METHOD

1. Define intent
2. Know Context
3. Know User
4. Frame insights

HOW TO USE THIS METHOD

McGahan concludes that industries changes as a result of two types of threats of obsolescence:

1. A threat to the industry's core activities
2. A threat to the industry's core assets

Organizations can react to change in these two areas in four ways

1. Radical when core assets and core activities are both threatened with obsolescence perform a balancing act
2. Progressive when neither core assets nor core activities are jeopardized
3. Creative when core assets are under threat but core activities are stable
4. Intermediating when core activities are threatened while core assets retain their capacity to create value

REFERENCES

1. McGahan, A. M. (2004). How Industries Evolve, Principles for Achieving and Sustaining Superior Performance. Boston, MA: Harvard Business School Press.
2. Rumelt, R. (1987), "Theory, Strategy, and Entrepreneurship," in D. Teece (Ed.) The Competitive Challenge: Strategies for Industrial Innovation and Renewal. Ballinger Publishing, Cambridge, MA.

VPEC-T

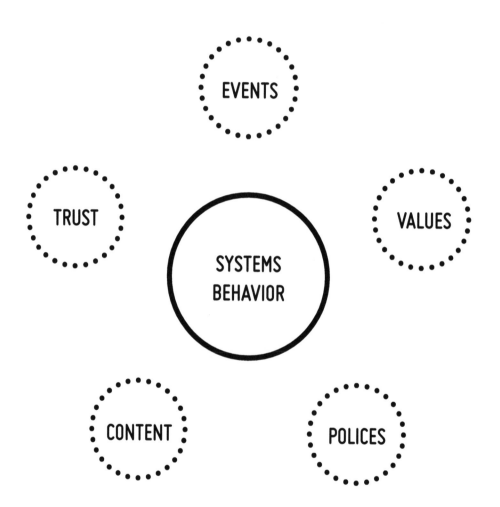

vpec-t

WHAT IS IT?

This technique is used when analyzing the expectations of people with different views who have an interest in common, but have different priorities and different responsibilities.

WHO INVENTED IT?

Nigel Green and Carl Bate, at Capgemini.

WHY USE THIS METHOD?

1. Vpec-t is used for information systems, mediation, communication and group interaction.
2. Establishing the requirements of a design from the different points of view of all parties involved;
3. Resolution of problems in a company with several groups performing similar business functions but with different policies.
4. Testing the likely success of options to change a business;

RESOURCES

1. Pen
2. Paper
3. White board
4. Dry erase markers
5. Post-it notes

WHEN TO USE THIS METHOD

1. Define intent

HOW TO USE THIS METHOD

These five filters are applied continuously during the early stages of considering a system: VPEC-T is a checklist for discussion.

1. Values The moral, objectives, desires and reservations of all stakeholders.
2. Policies Factors that may constrain the design in some way.
3. Events Things that happen.
4. Content The communications, and documents that are created through the business activity.
5. Trust – between stakeholders and users of the design.

REFERENCES

1. Graves, Tom (2008–12). "The Service-Oriented Enterprise: enterprise architecture and viable services". ISBN 09781906681166. Tetradian Books.

Chapter 4
Know people and context
what is needed?

active listening

WHAT IS IT?
Active listening is a communication method where the listener repeats what they understand to the speaker.

WHO INVENTED IT?
Thomas Gordon coined the term
Carl Rogers 1980

WHY USE THIS METHOD?
1. The ability to listen is an important skill for a designer to demonstrate empathy.

CHALLENGES
1. Listening and hearing or understanding are not the same
2. People give meaning to what they hear.
3. Listening constructs meaning from verbal and non verbal observations.

WHEN TO USE THIS METHOD
1. Know Context
2. Know User

HOW TO USE THIS METHOD
1. The listener observes the speakers body language.
2. This helps the listener understand the speaker's message
3. The listener paraphrases the speakers words to demonstrate understanding of the message.
4. The listener summarizes the issues.

Active listening skills include
1. Posture showing engagement
2. Eye contact
3. Environment that does not distract
4. Appropriate gestures and facial expressions.

REFERENCES
1. Reed, Warren H. (1985). Positive listening: learning to hear what people are really saying. New York: F. Watts. ISBN 0-531-09583-5
2. Atwater, Eastwood (1981). I Hear You. Prentice-Hall. p. 83. ISBN 0-13-450684-7.
3. Novack DH, Dube C, Goldstein MG. Teaching medical interviewing. A basic course on interviewing and the physician-patient relationship. Arch Intern Med 1992;152:1814—2.

activity analysis

WHAT IS IT?
Activity analysis is a method involving observing people in the context of their work.

WHO INVENTED IT?
Thomas Moran

WHY USE THIS METHOD?
1. Observation can reveal ways to make work more effective, efficient and valuable.

CHALLENGES
1. Medium level of cost and time required
2. Analysis may be difficult

WHEN TO USE THIS METHOD
3. Know Context
4. Know User
5. Frame insights

HOW TO USE THIS METHOD
1. Observe work in context
2. Undertake contextual interviews of workers
3. Analyze data
4. Create insights
5. Create Recommendations

RESOURCES
1. Note pad
2. Pens
3. Camera
4. Video camera
5. Digital voice recorder
6. Post-it notes

REFERENCES
1. Garrigou, A., Daniellous, F., Carballeda, G., Ruaud, S. Activity analysis in participatory design and analysis of participatory design activity.1995.

anthropometric analysis

WHAT IS IT?
It is a method of using statistical data about the distribution of body dimensions of people in order to optimize products and spaces.

WHO INVENTED IT?
Louis-Jean-Marie Daubenton 1784

WHY USE THIS METHOD?
Anthropometrics enables designers to properly size items, including system interfaces, to the "fit" the user.

CHALLENGES
1. All people are different but often one design will be used by many people.

RESOURCES
1. Human factors reference data

REFERENCES
1. Pheasant, Stephen (1986). Bodyspace : anthropometry, ergonomics, and design. London; Philadelphia: Taylor & Francis. ISBN 0-85066-352-0.
2. ISO 7250: Basic human body measurements for technological design, International Organization for Standardization, Humanscale 1-9 by Niels Diffrient, Alvin R. Tilley Published by MIT Press (MA) 1998 026204059X (ISBN13: 9780262040594)

Image Copyright Everett Collection, 2012
Used under license from Shutterstock.com

WHEN TO USE THIS METHOD
1. Define intent
2. Know Context
3. Know User
4. Frame insights
5. Explore Concepts

HOW TO USE THIS METHOD
1. Decide who you are designing for
2. Decide which body measurements are relevant
3. Decide whether you are designing for the 'average' or extremes. Consider whether the 5th, 50th, 95th or 100th percentile value may determine the boundaries of the design.
4. Consider Easy reach, A good match between the user and the product, A comfortable and safe posture, Easy and safe operation
5. You may need to add corrections for clothing. Does the user need to wear gloves?
6. You may also need to consider people's eyesight and hearing abilities.

anthropopump

WHAT IS IT?

This method involves the research videotaping one or more participant's activities. The videos are replayed to the participants and they are asked to explain their behavior.

WHO INVENTED IT?

Rick Robinson, John Cain, E- Lab Inc.,

WHY USE THIS METHOD?

1. Used for collecting data before concept and for evaluating prototypes after concept phases of projects,

CHALLENGES

1. Best conducted by someone who has practice observing human interactions in a space.

RESOURCES

1. Video camera
2. Video projector
3. Note pad
4. White board
5. Dry erase markers

WHEN TO USE THIS METHOD

1. Know Context
2. Know User
3. Frame insights

HOW TO USE THIS METHOD

1. People are first captured on video while interacting with products.
2. The participants are then asked to watch the tapes while researchers question them about what they see, how they felt, etc. In effect, research subjects analyses their own actions and experiences.
3. The company invites people who have been captured on video to watch their tapes as researchers pose questions about what's happening.
4. E Lab videotapes and dissects these follow-up sessions, analyzing research subjects analyzing themselves.

Source: [1]

REFERENCES

1. http://www.fastcompany.com/maga-zine/05/october-november-96

autoethnography

WHAT IS IT?
This is research where the researcher studies their own activities and behavior rather than others. May also refer to research of the cultural group that the researcher is part of.

WHO INVENTED IT?
Duncan 1993

WHY USE THIS METHOD?
1. Easy access to self
2. Inexpensive

CHALLENGES
1. Some quantitative researchers consider this method unscientific and unreliable.
2. The study may be too personal
3. May be difficult for the researcher to be objective when studying self.

WHEN TO USE THIS METHOD
4. Know Context
5. Know User
6. Frame insights

RESOURCES
1. Camera
2. Video camera
3. Note pad

HOW TO USE THIS METHOD
1. Be objective
2. Record data while the activity is being undertaken or soon after
3. Analyze and summarize data "
4. Create Reflexive journal summary

REFERENCES
1. Chang, Heewon. (2008). Autoethnography as method. Walnut Creek, CA: Left Coast Press.
2. Duncan, M., Autoethnography: Critical appreciation of an emerging art. International Journal of Qualitative Methods, 3, 4, (2004), Article 3,
3. Ellis, Carolyn. (2004). The Ethnographic I: A methodological novel about autoethnography. Walnut Creek: AltaMira Press.
4. Maréchal, Garance. (2010). Autoethnography. In Albert J. Mills, Gabrielle Durepos & Elden Wiebe (Eds.), Encyclopedia of case study research (Vol. 2, pp. 43-45). Thousand Oaks, CA: Sage Publications.

blind trials: single blind trial

WHAT IS IT?

He participants do not know if they are in the control or experimental group. The researchers know the test subjects role in the study,

WHO INVENTED IT?

Benjamin Franklin and Antoine Lavoisier, French Academy of Sciences 1784

WHY USE THIS METHOD?

1. Used to eliminate subjective bias by the subjects.

CHALLENGES

1. The tester could intentionally introduce bias

WHEN TO USE THIS METHOD

1. Know Context
2. Know User
3. Frame insights

HOW TO USE THIS METHOD

1. In a single-blind experiment, the participants do not know whether they are "test" subjects or members of an "experimental control" group
2. An example of a single-blind test is the "Pepsi challenge". A moderator has two cups one with Pepsi and one with a competitor's cola and asks a participant to identify the Pepsi. The participant does not know which cup contains the Pepsi.

REFERENCES

1. Friedman, L.M., Furberg, C.D., DeMets, D.L. (2010). Fundamentals of Clinical Trials. New York: Springer, pp. 119-132. ISBN 9781441915856

blind trials: double blind trial

WHAT IS IT?

He participants do not know if they are in the control or experimental group. The researchers do not know which group are subjects and which group is the control group in the study,

WHO INVENTED IT?

Benjamin Franklin and Antoine Lavoisier, French Academy of Sciences 1784

WHY USE THIS METHOD?

1. Used to eliminate subjective bias by both the participants and the research team.

CHALLENGES

1. The tester could intentionally introduce bias

WHEN TO USE THIS METHOD

1. Know Context
2. Know User
3. Frame insights

HOW TO USE THIS METHOD

1. In a single-blind experiment, the participants and the team administering the research do not know whether they are "test" subjects or members of an "experimental control" group

REFERENCES

1. Friedman, L.M., Furberg, C.D., DeMets, D.L. (2010). Fundamentals of Clinical Trials. New York: Springer, pp. 119–132. ISBN 9781441915856

case studies: clinical

WHAT IS IT?
A clinical case study is type of case study focuses on an individual person in depth. It often involves detailed interviews and observation.

WHO INVENTED IT?
Frederic Le Play is credited with creating the first case study in 1829

WHY USE THIS METHOD?
1. It is possible to uncover in-depth information.
2. It is flexible.
3. It can be undertaken in many different contexts.
4. It may be inexpensive.

CHALLENGES
1. You cannot generalize on the basis of an individual case
2. It is difficult to develop general theories on the basis of specific cases.
3. The case study has a bias toward confirming the researcher's preconceived notions.
4. Subjectivity
5. Time consuming

REFERENCES
1. Robert E. Stake, The Art of Case Study Research (Thousand Oaks: Sage, 1995). ISBN 0-8039-5767-X

WHEN TO USE THIS METHOD
1. Know Context
2. Know User
3. Frame insights

HOW TO USE THIS METHOD
1. Select the best type of case study for your audience.
2. Review similar case studies
3. Select your participants.
4. Determine whether you will study an individual or a group.
5. Draft a list of questions.
6. Arrange interviews
7. Obtain consent
8. Conduct interviews
9. Analyze the data
10. Create insights
11. Create recommendations.

RESOURCES
1. Note pad
2. Pens
3. Camera
4. Video camera
5. Digital audio recorder
6. Post-it notes

case studies: historical

WHAT IS IT?
Historical case studies follow the development of an individual, an institution, a system, a community, an organization, an event, or a culture over time.

WHO INVENTED IT?
Frederic Le Play is credited with creating the first case study in 1829

WHY USE THIS METHOD?
1. It is possible to uncover in-depth information.
2. It is flexible.
3. It can be undertaken in many different contexts.
4. It may be inexpensive.

CHALLENGES
1. You cannot generalize on the basis of an individual case
2. It is difficult to develop general theories on the basis of specific cases.
3. The case study has a bias toward confirming the researcher's preconceived notions.
4. Subjectivity
5. Time consuming

REFERENCES
1. Robert E. Stake, The Art of Case Study Research (Thousand Oaks: Sage, 1995). ISBN 0-8039-5767-X

WHEN TO USE THIS METHOD
1. Know Context
2. Know User
3. Frame insights

HOW TO USE THIS METHOD
1. Select the best type of case study for your audience.
2. Review similar case studies
3. Select your participants.
4. Determine whether you will study an individual or a group.
5. Draft a list of questions.
6. Arrange interviews
7. Obtain consent
8. Conduct interviews
9. Analyze the data
10. Create insights
11. Create recommendations.

RESOURCES
1. Note pad
2. Pens
3. Camera
4. Video camera
5. Digital audio recorder
6. Post-it notes

Image Copyright chippix, 2012
Used under license from Shutterstock.com

case studies: multi case

WHAT IS IT?
A multi-case study is a collection of case studies of an individual, an institution, a system, a community, an organization, an event, or a culture.

WHO INVENTED IT?
Frederic Le Play is credited with creating the first case study in 1829

WHY USE THIS METHOD?
1. It is possible to uncover in-depth information.
2. It is flexible.
3. It can be undertaken in many different contexts.
4. It may be inexpensive.

CHALLENGES
1. You cannot generalize on the basis of an individual case
2. It is difficult to develop general theories on the basis of specific cases.
3. The case study has a bias toward confirming the researcher's preconceived notions.
4. Subjectivity
5. Time consuming

Image Copyright Igor Dutina, 2012
Used under license from Shutterstock.com

WHEN TO USE THIS METHOD
1. Know Context
2. Know User
3. Frame insights

HOW TO USE THIS METHOD
1. Select the best type of case study for your audience.
2. Review similar case studies
3. Select your participants.
4. Determine whether you will study an individual or a group.
5. Draft a list of questions.
6. Arrange interviews
7. Obtain consent
8. Conduct interviews
9. Analyze the data
10. Create insights
11. Create recommendations.

RESOURCES
1. Note pad
2. Pens
3. Camera
4. Video camera
5. Digital audio recorder
6. Post-it notes

REFERENCES
1. Robert E. Stake, The Art of Case Study Research (Thousand Oaks: Sage, 1995). ISBN 0-8039-5767-X
2. "Case Study," in Norman K. Denzin and Yvonna S. Lincoln, eds., The Sage Handbook of Qualitative Research, 4th Edition (Thousand Oaks, CA: Sage),

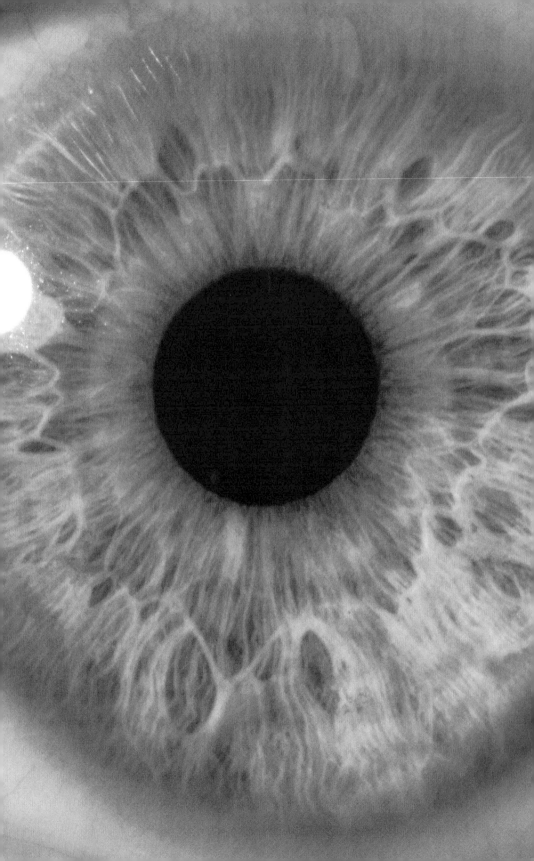

case studies: observational

WHAT IS IT?
Observational case studies focus on observing an individual, an institution, a system, a community, an organization, an event, or a culture.

WHO INVENTED IT?
Frederic Le Play is credited with creating the first case study in 1829

WHY USE THIS METHOD?
1. It is possible to uncover in-depth information.
2. It is flexible.
3. It can be undertaken in many different contexts.
4. It may be inexpensive.

CHALLENGES
1. You cannot generalize on the basis of an individual case
2. It is difficult to develop general theories on the basis of specific cases.
3. The case study has a bias toward confirming the researcher's preconceived notions.
4. Subjectivity
5. Time consuming

WHEN TO USE THIS METHOD
1. Know Context
2. Know User
3. Frame insights

HOW TO USE THIS METHOD
1. Select the best type of case study for your audience.
2. Review similar case studies
3. Select your participants.
4. Determine whether you will study an individual or a group.
5. Obtain consent
6. Conduct observations
7. Analyze the data
8. Create insights
9. Create recommendations.

RESOURCES
1. Note pad
2. Pens
3. Camera
4. Video camera
5. Digital audio recorder
6. Post-it notes

REFERENCES
1. Robert E. Stake, The Art of Case Study Research (Thousand Oaks: Sage, 1995). ISBN 0-8039-5767-X
2. "Case Study," in Norman K. Denzin and Yvonna S. Lincoln, eds., The Sage Handbook of Qualitative Research, 4th Edition (Thousand Oaks, CA: Sage),

case studies: oral history

WHAT IS IT?

Oral case studies are case studies narrated by one person speaking for and about themselves. This allows communication of their point of view. The narrator may or may not be aware of the full context of their experiences.

WHO INVENTED IT?

Frederic Le Play is credited with creating the first case study in 1829

WHY USE THIS METHOD?

1. It is possible to uncover in-depth information.
2. It is flexible.
3. It can be undertaken in many different contexts.
4. It may be inexpensive.

CHALLENGES

1. You cannot generalize on the basis of an individual case
2. It is difficult to develop general theories on the basis of specific cases.
3. The case study has a bias toward confirming the researcher's preconceived notions.
4. Subjectivity
5. Time consuming

Image Copyright dundanim, 2012
Used under license from Shutterstock.com

WHEN TO USE THIS METHOD

1. Know Context
2. Know User
3. Frame insights

HOW TO USE THIS METHOD

1. Select the best type of case study for your audience.
2. Review similar case studies
3. Select your participants.
4. Determine whether you will study an individual or a group.
5. Draft a list of questions.
6. Arrange interviews
7. Conduct interviews
8. Analyze the data
9. Create insights
10. Create recommendations.

RESOURCES

1. Note pad
2. Pens
3. Camera
4. Video camera
5. Digital audio recorder
6. Post-it notes

REFERENCES

1. Robert E. Stake, The Art of Case Study Research (Thousand Oaks: Sage, 1995). ISBN 0-8039-5767-X
2. "Case Study," in Norman K. Denzin and Yvonna S. Lincoln, eds., The Sage Handbook of Qualitative Research, 4th Edition (Thousand Oaks, CA: Sage),

case studies: situational

WHAT IS IT?
This form studies particular events. The view of all participants in the event are sought

WHO INVENTED IT?
Frederic Le Play is credited with creating the first case study in 1829

WHY USE THIS METHOD?
1. It is possible to uncover in-depth information.
2. It is flexible.
3. It can be undertaken in many different contexts.
4. It may be inexpensive.

CHALLENGES
1. You cannot generalize on the basis of an individual case
2. It is difficult to develop general theories on the basis of specific cases.
3. The case study has a bias toward confirming the researcher's preconceived notions.
4. Subjectivity
5. Time consuming

REFERENCES
1. Robert E. Stake, The Art of Case Study Research (Thousand Oaks: Sage, 1995). ISBN 0-8039-5767-X
2. "Case Study," in Norman K. Denzin and Yvonna S. Lincoln, eds., The Sage Handbook of Qualitative Research, 4th Edition (Thousand Oaks, CA: Sage),

WHEN TO USE THIS METHOD
1. Know Context
2. Know User
3. Frame insights

HOW TO USE THIS METHOD
1. Select the best type of case study for your audience.
2. Review similar case studies
3. Select your participants.
4. Determine whether you will study an individual or a group.
5. Draft a list of questions.
6. Arrange interviews
7. Obtain consent
8. Conduct interviews
9. Analyze the data
10. Create insights
11. Create recommendations.

RESOURCES
1. Note pad
2. Pens
3. Camera
4. Video camera
5. Digital audio recorder
6. Post-it notes

Image Copyright Joe Gough, 2012
Used under license from Shutterstock.com

close ended questions

WHAT IS IT?

Close ended questions are questions that can be answered with simple yes or no responses or a specific answer that doesn't need to be interpreted. Also called dichotomous or saturated questions.

Some examples are:
1. Shall we continue?
2. Is this correct?
3. What is this color?

WHY USE THIS METHOD?
1. Fast
2. Easy to analyze answers

CHALLENGES
1. Should be used in an interview to clarify responses.
2. Should be combined with open ended questions.
3. Can be leading.
4. Open-ended questions develop trust
5. Perceived as more threatening than open ended questions.
6. A closed question may be impossible to answer such as "Have you stopped taking cocaine?"

WHEN TO USE THIS METHOD
1. Know Context
2. Know User

HOW TO USE THIS METHOD
1. If people stop responding to open questions ask close ended questions to restart conversation.
2. Multiple choice questions are a form of closed question.

RESOURCES
1. Pen
2. Paper
3. Video camera
4. Question guide
5. Digital voice recorder
6. Questionnaires
7. Surveys

REFERENCES
1. Dillman D., Smyth J., & Christioan LM. (2009) Internet and Mixed-Mode Surveys. The Tailored Design Method. John Wiley & Sons. New Jersey.
2. Howard Schuman and Stanley Presser (October 1979). "The Open and Closed Question". American Sociological Review 44 (5): 692–712.

CONJOINT ANALYSIS

Please rate how you like these types of cheese

	I really dislike it	I do not like it	Neutral	I like it	I like it a lot
Cheddar	☐	☐	☐	☐	☐
Stilton	☐	☐	☐	☐	☐
Danish Blue	☐	☐	☐	☐	☐
Gorgonzola	☐	☐	☐	☐	☐

conjoint analysis

WHAT IS IT?
Conjoint analysis is a method to gain insight into how people value features or components of a product , service or experience. It can be used to decide features a new product should have and how a new product should be priced.

WHO INVENTED IT?
Paul Green University of Pennsylvania.
V. "Seenu" Srinivasan Stanford University

WHY USE THIS METHOD?
1. Uncovers perceptions that the respondent may not be consciously aware of.
2. Can use physical objects.
3. Attempts to measure psychological trade-offs when evaluating several attributes together
4. Can be carried out telephone or face-to-face.

CHALLENGES
1. Studies can be complex

RESOURCES
1. Paper
2. Pens
3. Phone
4. Questionnaires
5. Software

WHEN TO USE THIS METHOD
1. Define intent
2. Know Context
3. Know User
4. Frame insights

HOW TO USE THIS METHOD
1. The respondent is shown a number of features sometimes in pairs
2. The respondent rates or chooses combinations of features.
3. The data is analyzed and the features ranked.
4. Mathematical models are used to determine the respondent's product or service of choice.

REFERENCES
1. Green, P. and Srinivasan, V. (1978) Conjoint analysis in consumer research: Issues and outlook, Journal of Consumer Research, vol 5, September 1978, pp 103-123.
2. Orme, B. (2005) Getting Started with Conjoint Analysis Madison, WI: Research Publishers LLC. ISBN 0-9727297-4-7
3. Louviere, Jordan J. "Conjoint Analysis Modelling of Stated Preferences: A Review of Theory, Methods, Recent Developments and External Validity." Journal of Transport Economics and Policy, Vol. 22, No. 1, Stated Preference Methods in Transport Research (Jan., 1988), pp. 93-119.

customer first questions

WHAT IS IT?
Customer first questions predict the reaction of customers to a new product or service.

WHO INVENTED IT?
Edith Wilson, Hewlett-Packard,

WHY USE THIS METHOD?
1. To identify customer needs and desires.
2. To reduce the risk of product development
3. To reduce the number of product design changes during the development process.
4. The Customer first questions method has been used by many large organizations

WHEN TO USE THIS METHOD
1. Define intent
2. Know Context
3. Know User
4. Frame insights

HOW TO USE THIS METHOD
1. Brainstorm the most appropriate research methods.
   - What customer problems does our product/service solve that our competitors do not?
   - What benefits does our product/service offer that our competitors do not?
   - What motivates the customer to purchase our product/service over that of our competitors?
2. Identify using research the needs and desires of customers.
3. Analyze how the product satisfies these needs and desired and how this compares to competitor's products.
4. Analyze whether customers will prefer the product to competitor's products.

RESOURCES
1. Paper
2. Pens
3. White board
4. Dry erase markers

CUSTOMER NEEDS MATRIX

	CUSTOMER DEMOGRAPHICS	CUSTOMER NEEDS	USAGE				
			WHO	WHAT	WHEN	WHERE	HOW
1							
2							
3							
4							
5							
6							
7							
8							
9							
10							
11							
12							

customer needs matrix

WHAT IS IT?

The customer needs table helps integrated product development teams (IPDT) translate customer needs and wants into required designs that may meet customer expectations prior to the potential development of new products or service development.

WHY USE THIS METHOD?

1. To uncover customer needs and desires
2. To translate customer needs and desires into product features.
3. To reduce changes necessary during product development.

RESOURCES

1. Paper
2. Pens
3. White board
4. Dry erase markers

WHEN TO USE THIS METHOD

1. Define intent
2. Know Context
3. Know User
4. Frame insights

HOW TO USE THIS METHOD

1. The design team selects methods for collecting data.
2. Data collection methods : Customer surveys, interviews, focus groups, benchmarks, similar product data, summarized studies, product demos, and others.
3. A sample of customers is selected and interviewed in relation to the factors listed on the customer needs matrix.
4. The responses are entered into the table.
5. The table is reviewed by the team.
6. The team creates a list of insights.

DEMING CYCLE

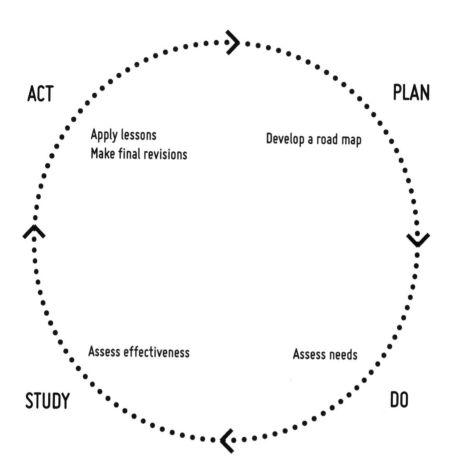

ACT

Apply lessons
Make final revisions

PLAN

Develop a road map

STUDY

Assess effectiveness

DO

Assess needs

deming cycle

WHAT IS IT?

The Deming Cycle is a method to test information before making a decision for the continuous improvement of systems and products. Also known as PDCA and Shewhart cycle. A principal of the method is iteration.

WHO INVENTED IT?

Made popular by Dr. W. Edwards Deming based on the "scientific method"of Francis Bacon *Novum Organum, 1620*

WHY USE THIS METHOD?

1.   To assess proposed problem solutions
2.   To identify and measure the effects and outcomes of initial, trial efforts.

RESOURCES

1.   Paper
2.   Pens
3.   White board
4.   Dry erase markers

WHEN TO USE THIS METHOD

1.   Frame insights
2.   Explore Concepts

HOW TO USE THIS METHOD

Plan. Establish objectives.
Do. Implement the plan.
Check. Study the results and compare to the expected results.
Act. On differences between planned and actual results.

REFERENCES

1.   Rother, Mike (2010). Toyota Kata. Chapter 6: MGraw-Hill. ISBN 978-0-07-163523-3.

dramaturgy

WHAT IS IT?
Dramaturgy is a method that uses drama techniques to help understand user behaviors and needs. It a form of prototyping.

WHO INVENTED IT?
Robert, Benford D., and Scott A. Hunt

WHY USE THIS METHOD?
1. Created to make personas more dynamic.

CHALLENGES
1. Some team members may be uncomfortable with drama based activity.
2. The method is not in context
3. The method may be subjective as it does not involve the people being designed for,

WHEN TO USE THIS METHOD
4. Know Context
5. Know User
6. Frame insights
7. Explore Concepts

HOW TO USE THIS METHOD
1. Choose a character
2. Create groups of 2 or 3 members of your design team
3. Ask your teams to write monologues for the characters based on public, private and intimate levels.
4. Ask your team to discuss the rituals of the character's lives
5. Ask your team to create maps of the stakeholders
6. Create scenes exploring crucial moments in your character's experiences or interactions.
7. Present these scenarios with groups of actors.
8. Explore the problems and challenges of the character's experiences and interactions.

REFERENCES
1. Robert, Benford D., and Scott A. Hunt. "Dramaturgy and Social Movements: The Social Construction and Communication of Power." Social Inquiry 62.1 (2007): 36-55. Wiley Online Library.

drawing experiences

WHAT IS IT?

This method involves asking respondents to create drawings to illustrate their experiences.

WHO INVENTED IT?

Used by design consultants IDEO

WHY USE THIS METHOD?

1. Drawing can elicit information difficult for respondents to describe in words.

CHALLENGES

1. A drawing of an experience is different to an experience which involves all senses.
2. Some people are not confident expressing themselves through drawing.

WHEN TO USE THIS METHOD

1. Know Context
2. Know User
3. Frame insights

HOW TO USE THIS METHOD

1. Select a moderator
2. Select a group of 4 to 12 users
3. Ask users to create an image of an experience through a drawing.

RESOURCES

1. Pens
2. Paper

REFERENCES

1. IDEO method cards. Publication Date: November 2003 ISBN-10: 0954413210 ISBN-13: 978-0954413217

ethnocentrism

WHAT IS IT?

Ethnocentrism is a characteristic of human behavior that can stand in the way of creating effective design solutions. As designers are working increasingly on global projects ethnocentrism is becoming something which needs to be more carefully considered. Ethnocentrism is judging another culture only by the values and standards of one's own culture. Ethnocentrism leads to misunderstanding others. We falsely distort what is meaningful and functional to other peoples through our own tinted glasses

WHO INVENTED IT?

William G. Sumner first used the term

WHY USE THIS METHOD?

1. Ethnocentrism can lead to failed design efforts.
2. Ethnocentrism can lead to conflicts.

CHALLENGES

1. It is useful to recognize ethnocentrism when designing across cultures and to make efforts to reduce it's impact on the outcomes of a project.

WHEN TO USE THIS METHOD

1. Define intent
2. Know Context
3. Know User
4. Frame insights
5. Explore Concepts

TO REDUCE ETHNOCENTRISM

1. Recognize that we do not understand, that we are falsely assuming something that is not the case and is out of context.
2. Control our biases and to seek more valid and balanced understanding.
3. Ask "How are the behaviors meaningful and functional to the people being studied?"
4. When we encounter ethnocentrism being promoted by particular groups, we can ask ourselves and those around us "Why are they doing this?" What function does promoting ethnocentrism

REFERENCES

1. Ankerl, G. Coexisting Contemporary Civilizations: Arabo-Muslim, Bharati, Chinese, and Western. Geneva: INU PRESS, 2000, ISBN 2-88155-004-5
2. Reynolds, V., Falger, V., & Vine, I. (Eds.) (1987). The Sociobiology of Ethnocentrism. Athens, GA: University of Georgia Press.
3. Shimp, Terence. Sharma, Shubhash. "Consumer Ethnocentrism: Construction and Validation of the CETSCALE. Journal of Marketing Research. 24 (3). Aug 1987.

explore represent share

WHAT IS IT?

This is a process for designing your own user research methods. It is a structured group facilitation process.

WHO INVENTED IT?

Denis O'Brien

WHEN TO USE THIS METHOD

1. Explore Concepts

HOW TO USE THIS METHOD

1. Participants are encouraged to explore ideas, represent them in words, drawings and objects and share their meanings.
2. The moderator prompts respondents with written questions to document their thoughts on paper.
3. Some sample prompts are:
"My ideal research method would be."
"This wouldn't work because."
4. Participants interpret each others output.
5. When we encounter ethnocentrism being promoted by particular groups, we can ask ourselves and those around us "Why are they doing this?" What function does promoting ethnocentrism

RESOURCES

1. Pens
2. Paper
3. Video camera
4. Digital voice recorder
5. Forms

REFERENCES

1. O'Brien, Denis. The Methods Lab: Explore, Represent, Share.
2. Koberg, Don, Bagnall, Jim. The Universal Traveler: a Soft-Systems guide to creativity, problem-solving, and the process of reaching goals.
3. J. Christopher Jones, Design Methods (New York: Van Nostrand Reinhold, 1992).

field experiment

WHAT IS IT?
A field experiment is an experiment conducted outside the laboratory, in a 'natural' context This method often involves changing one or more variables in a context to understand their effect and randomizing participants into treatment and control groups.

WHO INVENTED IT?
Abu Rayman al-Biruni 1030 AD

WHY USE THIS METHOD?
1. Because the settings are more natural it is assumed that people will behave more naturally
2. Less sample bias.
3. Fewer demand characteristics if participants are unaware.
4. Designers conduct field experiments with prototypes to obtain feedback and refine designs.

CHALLENGES
1. Difficult to replicate
2. Informed consent may be difficult to obtain.
3. Less control of variables
4. Difficult to replicate.
5. Difficult to record data accurately.
6. If participants are unaware of the study how can the consent to take part or withdraw from the experiment?
7. Many participants are required to make reliable claims

WHEN TO USE THIS METHOD
1. Know Context
2. Know User
3. Frame insights

HOW TO USE THIS METHOD
Various methods are possible
Consider:
1. What resources are available
2. What will you test and compare?
3. What will be your methods?
4. How will you gain access and participation?

RESOURCES
1. Note pad
2. Pens
3. Camera
4. Video camera
5. Digital voice recorder

REFERENCES
1. Reichardt, C. S. & Mark, M. M. (2004). Quasi-Experimentation. In J. S. Wholey, H. P. Hatry, & K. E. Newcomber (Eds.) Handbook of Practical Program Evaluation, Second Edition, San Franciso: Jossey-Bass.

focus group: client participant

WHAT IS IT?

A client participant focus group allows the client to participate either visibly or invisibly through a one way mirror. This method allows the client to interpret the answers and the a participant's body language and to ensure that the discussion covers what the client would like to be covered.

WHO INVENTED IT?

Robert K. Merton 1940 Bureau of Applied Social Research.

WHY USE THIS METHOD?

1. A focus group allows an in depth probe.
2. Interaction between participants can uncover broader insights.
3. They are cost effective for the volume and quality of data
4. Are less expensive than conducting 8 to 12 in depth interviews
5. Are time efficient
6. Clients can gain insights by observing the group interaction through a one way mirror.

CHALLENGES

1. Participants can influence each other.
2. Data is not quantifiable.
3. Responses are limited.
4. Data may be difficult to analyze
5. The participants are out of the context of their usual environments.

WHEN TO USE THIS METHOD

1. Know Context
2. Know User
3. Frame insights
4. Explore Concepts

HOW TO USE THIS METHOD

1. Focus groups often take one and a half to two hours.
2. Ask 5 to 10 questions.
3. Define purpose
4. Ask:
   ° Why a focus group?
   ° Who are the stakeholders?
   ° Who is the target population?
   ° What problems will be explored?
5. Define resources
6. Write question guide.
7. Recruit participants.
8. Conduct focus group.
9. Analyze data.
10. Create insights.
11. Take actions.

RESOURCES

1. Focus group space.
2. Sound and video recording equipment
3. White board
4. Pens
5. Post-it-notes

REFERENCES

1. Nachmais, Chava Frankfort; Nachmais, David. 2008. Research methods in the Social Sciences: Seventh Edition New York, NY: Worth Publishers

focus group: devil's advocate

WHAT IS IT?

This with method two moderators present contrary viewpoints. The different ways of thinking provide new insights.

WHO INVENTED IT?

Robert K. Merton 1940 Bureau of Applied Social Research.

WHY USE THIS METHOD?

1. A focus group allows an in depth probe.
2. Interaction between participants can uncover broader insights.
3. They are cost effective for the volume and quality of data
4. Are less expensive than conducting 8 to 12 in depth interviews
5. Are time efficient
6. Clients can gain insights by observing the group interaction through a one way mirror.

CHALLENGES

1. Participants can influence each other.
2. Data is not quantifiable.
3. Responses are limited.
4. Data may be difficult to analyze
5. The participants are out of the context of their usual environments.

WHEN TO USE THIS METHOD

1. Know Context
2. Know User
3. Frame insights
4. Explore Concepts

HOW TO USE THIS METHOD

1. Focus groups often take one and a half to two hours.
2. Ask 5 to 10 questions.
3. Define purpose
4. Ask:
   ◦ Why a focus group?
   ◦ Who are the stakeholders?
   ◦ Who is the target population?
   ◦ What problems will be explored?
5. Define resources
6. Write question guide.
7. Recruit participants.
8. Conduct focus group.
9. Analyze data.
10. Create insights.
11. Take actions.

RESOURCES

1. Focus group space.
2. Sound and video recording equipment
3. White board
4. Pens
5. Post-it-notes

REFERENCES

1. Nachmais, Chava Frankfort; Nachmais, David. 2008. Research methods in the Social Sciences: Seventh Edition New York, NY: Worth Publishers

focus group: dual moderator

WHAT IS IT?
The dual moderator focus group involves two moderators. One moderator manages the time progression. The second moderator ensures that the discussion remains on the focus topics.

WHO INVENTED IT?
Robert K. Merton 1940 Bureau of Applied Social Research.

WHY USE THIS METHOD?
1. A focus group allows an in depth probe.
2. Interaction between participants can uncover broader insights.
3. They are cost effective for the volume and quality of data
4. Are less expensive than conducting 8 to 12 in depth interviews
5. Are time efficient
6. Clients can gain insights by observing the group interaction through a one way mirror.

CHALLENGES
1. Participants can influence each other.
2. Data is not quantifiable.
3. Responses are limited.
4. Data may be difficult to analyze
5. The participants are out of the context of their usual environments.

WHEN TO USE THIS METHOD
1. Know Context
2. Know User
3. Frame insights
4. Explore Concepts

HOW TO USE THIS METHOD
1. Focus groups often take one and a half to two hours.
2. Ask 5 to 10 questions.
3. Define purpose
4. Ask:
   ◦ Why a focus group?
   ◦ Who are the stakeholders?
   ◦ Who is the target population?
   ◦ What problems will be explored?
5. Define resources
6. Write question guide.
7. Recruit participants.
8. Conduct focus group.
9. Analyze data.
10. Create insights.
11. Take actions.

RESOURCES
1. Focus group space.
2. Sound and video recording equipment
3. White board
4. Pens
5. Post-it-notes

REFERENCES
1. Nachmais, Chava Frankfort; Nachmais, David. 2008. Research methods in the Social Sciences: Seventh Edition New York, NY: Worth Publishers

focus group: mini focus group

WHAT IS IT?
A mini focus group has four or five participants. Other methods commonly involve eight to twelve participants. This method may be appropriate for exploring more intimate or sensitive subjects.

WHO INVENTED IT?
Robert K. Merton 1940 Bureau of Applied Social Research.

WHY USE THIS METHOD?
1. A focus group allows an in depth probe.
2. Interaction between participants can uncover broader insights.
3. They are cost effective for the volume and quality of data
4. Are less expensive than conducting 8 to 12 in depth interviews
5. Are time efficient
6. Clients can gain insights by observing the group interaction through a one way mirror.

CHALLENGES
1. Participants can influence each other.
2. Data is not quantifiable.
3. Responses are limited.
4. Data may be difficult to analyze
5. The participants are out of the context of their usual environments.

WHEN TO USE THIS METHOD
1. Know Context
2. Know User
3. Frame insights
4. Explore Concepts

HOW TO USE THIS METHOD
1. Focus groups often take one and a half to two hours.
2. Ask 5 to 10 questions.
3. Define purpose
4. Ask:
   - Why a focus group?
   - Who are the stakeholders?
   - Who is the target population?
   - What problems will be explored?
5. Define resources
6. Write question guide.
7. Recruit participants.
8. Conduct focus group.
9. Analyze data.
10. Create insights.
11. Take actions.

RESOURCES
1. Focus group space.
2. Sound and video recording equipment
3. White board
4. Pens
5. Post-it-notes

REFERENCES
1. Nachmais, Chava Frankfort; Nachmais, David. 2008. Research methods in the Social Sciences: Seventh Edition New York, NY: Worth Publishers

focus group: online

WHAT IS IT?
This is a focus group where the participants are involved from different locations via their computers.

WHO INVENTED IT?
Robert K. Merton 1940 Bureau of Applied Social Research.

WHY USE THIS METHOD?
1. A focus group allows an in depth probe.
2. Interaction between participants can uncover broader insights.
3. They are cost effective for the volume and quality of data
4. Are less expensive than conducting 8 to 12 in depth interviews
5. Are time efficient
6. Clients can gain insights by observing the group interaction through a one way mirror.

CHALLENGES
1. Participants can influence each other.
2. Data is not quantifiable.
3. Responses are limited.
4. Data may be difficult to analyze
5. The participants are out of the context of their usual environments.

WHEN TO USE THIS METHOD
1. Know Context
2. Know User
3. Frame insights
4. Explore Concepts

HOW TO USE THIS METHOD
1. Define purpose
2. Ask:
   ◦ Why a focus group?
   ◦ Who are the stakeholders?
   ◦ Who is the target population?
   ◦ What problems will be explored?
3. Define resources
4. Write question guide.
5. Recruit participants.
6. Conduct focus group.
7. Analyze data.
8. Create insights.
9. Take actions.

RESOURCES
1. Focus group space.
2. Sound and video recording equipment
3. White board
4. Pens
5. Post-it-notes

REFERENCES
1. Nachmais, Chava Frankfort; Nachmais, David. 2008. Research methods in the Social Sciences: Seventh Edition New York, NY: Worth Publishers

focus group: other participant

WHAT IS IT?
One or more selected people participate as a group member or moderator in the discussion temporarily or for the full duration. This may be an expert such as the designer, writer, or some other specialist.

WHO INVENTED IT?
Robert K. Merton 1940 Bureau of Applied Social Research.

WHY USE THIS METHOD?
1. A focus group allows an in depth probe.
2. Interaction between participants can uncover broader insights.
3. They are cost effective for the volume and quality of data
4. Are less expensive than conducting 8 to 12 in depth interviews
5. Are time efficient
6. Clients can gain insights by observing the group interaction through a one way mirror.

CHALLENGES
1. Participants can influence each other.
2. Data is not quantifiable.
3. Responses are limited.
4. Data may be difficult to analyze
5. The participants are out of the context of their usual environments.

WHEN TO USE THIS METHOD
1. Know Context
2. Know User
3. Frame insights
4. Explore Concepts

HOW TO USE THIS METHOD
1. Focus groups often take one and a half to two hours.
2. Ask:
   ◦ Why a focus group?
   ◦ Who are the stakeholders?
   ◦ Who is the target population?
   ◦ What problems will be explored?
3. Define resources
4. Write question guide.
5. Recruit participants.
6. Conduct focus group.
7. Analyze data.
8. Create insights.
9. Take actions.

RESOURCES
1. Focus group space.
2. Sound and video recording equipment
3. White board
4. Pens
5. Post-it-notes

REFERENCES
1. Nachmais, Chava Frankfort; Nachmais, David. 2008. Research methods in the Social Sciences: Seventh Edition New York, NY: Worth Publishers

focus group: respondent moderator

WHAT IS IT?
A respondent moderator focus group involves the participants and moderator exchanging roles. A diversity of viewpoints from a number of different moderators results in more honest diverse responses

WHO INVENTED IT?
Robert K. Merton 1940 Bureau of Applied Social Research.

WHY USE THIS METHOD?
1. A focus group allows an in depth probe.
2. Interaction between participants can uncover broader insights.
3. They are cost effective for the volume and quality of data
4. Are less expensive than conducting 8 to 12 in depth interviews
5. Are time efficient
6. Clients can gain insights by observing the group interaction through a one way mirror.

CHALLENGES
1. Participants can influence each other.
2. Data is not quantifiable.
3. Responses are limited.
4. Data may be difficult to analyze
5. The participants are out of the context of their usual environments.

WHEN TO USE THIS METHOD
1. Know Context
2. Know User
3. Frame insights
4. Explore Concepts

HOW TO USE THIS METHOD
1. Focus groups often take one and a half to two hours.
2. Ask 5 to 10 questions.
3. Define purpose
4. Ask:
° Why a focus group?
° Who are the stakeholders?
° Who is the target population?
° What problems will be explored?
5. Define resources
6. Write question guide.
7. Recruit participants.
8. Conduct focus group.
9. Analyze data.
10. Create insights.
11. Take actions.

RESOURCES
1. Focus group space.
2. Sound and video recording equipment
3. White board
4. Pens
5. Post-it-notes

REFERENCES
1. Nachmais, Chava Frankfort; Nachmais, David. 2008. Research methods in the Social Sciences: Seventh Edition New York, NY: Worth Publishers

focus group: structured

WHAT IS IT?

With a structured focus group each question has a pre determined time for discussion and when this time is reached the moderator moves the group onto the next question for discussion.

WHO INVENTED IT?

Robert K. Merton 1940 Bureau of Applied Social Research.

WHY USE THIS METHOD?

1. A focus group allows an in depth probe.
2. Interaction between participants can uncover broader insights.
3. They are cost effective for the volume and quality of data
4. Are less expensive than conducting 8 to 12 in depth interviews
5. Are time efficient
6. Clients can gain insights by observing the group interaction through a one way mirror.

CHALLENGES

1. Participants can influence each other.
2. Data is not quantifiable.
3. Responses are limited.
4. Data may be difficult to analyze
5. The participants are out of the context of their usual environments.

WHEN TO USE THIS METHOD

1. Know Context
2. Know User
3. Frame insights
4. Explore Concepts

HOW TO USE THIS METHOD

1. Focus groups often take one and a half to two hours.
2. Ask:
  - Why a focus group?
  - Who are the stakeholders?
  - Who is the target population?
  - What problems will be explored?
3. Define resources
4. Write question guide.
5. Recruit participants.
6. Conduct focus group.
7. Analyze data.
8. Create insights.
9. Take actions.

RESOURCES

1. Focus group space.
2. Sound and video recording equipment
3. White board
4. Pens
5. Post-it-notes

REFERENCES

1. Nachmais, Chava Frankfort; Nachmais, David. 2008. Research methods in the Social Sciences: Seventh Edition New York, NY: Worth Publishers

focus group: teleconference

WHAT IS IT?
This method involves conducting a focus group via teleconference. It allows participation at lower cost from diverse geographical locations.

WHY USE THIS METHOD?
1. A focus group allows an in depth probe.
2. Interaction between participants can uncover broader insights.
3. They are cost effective for the volume and quality of data
4. Are less expensive than conducting 8 to 12 in depth interviews
5. Are time efficient
6. Clients can gain insights by observing the group interaction through a one way mirror.

CHALLENGES
1. Participants cannot read each other's body language.
2. Participants can influence each other.
3. Data is not quantifiable.
4. Responses are limited.
5. Data may be difficult to analyze
6. The participants are out of the context of their usual environments.

WHEN TO USE THIS METHOD
1. Know Context
2. Know User
3. Frame insights
4. Explore Concepts

HOW TO USE THIS METHOD
1. Define purpose
2. Ask:
   ◦ Why a focus group?
   ◦ Who are the stakeholders?
   ◦ Who is the target population?
   ◦ What problems will be explored?
3. Define resources
4. Write question guide.
5. Recruit participants.
6. Conduct focus group.
7. Analyze data.
8. Create insights.
9. Take actions.

RESOURCES
1. Focus group space.
2. Sound and video recording equipment
3. White board
4. Pens
5. Post-it-notes

REFERENCES
1. Nachmais, Chava Frankfort; Nachmais, David. 2008. Research methods in the Social Sciences: Seventh Edition New York, NY: Worth Publishers

focus group: two way

WHAT IS IT?
With this method there are two groups of participants. One group watches the other group's responses. The second group will have different discussions and conclusions based on the first group's responses.

WHO INVENTED IT?
Robert K. Merton 1940 Bureau of Applied Social Research.

WHY USE THIS METHOD?
1. A focus group allows an in depth probe.
2. Interaction between participants can uncover broader insights.
3. They are cost effective for the volume and quality of data
4. Are less expensive than conducting 8 to 12 in depth interviews
5. Are time efficient
6. Clients can gain insights by observing the group interaction through a one way mirror.

CHALLENGES
1. Participants can influence each other.
2. Data is not quantifiable.
3. Responses are limited.
4. Data may be difficult to analyze
5. The participants are out of the context of their usual environments.

WHEN TO USE THIS METHOD
1. Know Context
2. Know User
3. Frame insights
4. Explore Concepts

HOW TO USE THIS METHOD
1. Focus groups often take one and a half to two hours.
2. Ask 5 to 10 questions.
3. Define purpose
4. Ask:
   ◦ Why a focus group?
   ◦ Who are the stakeholders?
   ◦ Who is the target population?
   ◦ What problems will be explored?
5. Define resources
6. Write question guide.
7. Recruit participants.
8. Conduct focus group.
9. Analyze data.
10. Create insights.
11. Take actions.

RESOURCES
1. Focus group space.
2. Sound and video recording equipment
3. White board
4. Pens
5. Post-it-notes

REFERENCES
1. Nachmais, Chava Frankfort; Nachmais, David. 2008. Research methods in the Social Sciences: Seventh Edition New York, NY: Worth Publishers

focus group: unstructured

WHAT IS IT?

An unstructured focus group has flexible moderation. The moderator allows conversations to go in different directions and may allow more time for discussion if required to explore topics.

WHO INVENTED IT?

Robert K. Merton 1940 Bureau of Applied Social Research.

WHY USE THIS METHOD?

1. A focus group allows an in depth probe.
2. Interaction between participants can uncover broader insights.
3. They are cost effective for the volume and quality of data
4. Are less expensive than conducting 8 to 12 in depth interviews
5. Are time efficient
6. Clients can gain insights by observing the group interaction through a one way mirror.

CHALLENGES

1. Participants can influence each other.
2. Data is not quantifiable.
3. Responses are limited.
4. Data may be difficult to analyze
5. The participants are out of the context of their usual environments.

WHEN TO USE THIS METHOD

1. Know Context
2. Know User
3. Frame insights
4. Explore Concepts

HOW TO USE THIS METHOD

1. Focus groups often take one and a half to two hours.
2. Ask:
   ° Why a focus group?
   ° Who are the stakeholders?
   ° Who is the target population?
   ° What problems will be explored?
3. Define resources
4. Write question guide.
5. Recruit participants.
6. Conduct focus group.
7. Analyze data.
8. Create insights.
9. Take actions.

RESOURCES

1. Focus group space.
2. Sound and video recording equipment
3. White board
4. Pens
5. Post-it-notes

REFERENCES

1. Nachmais, Chava Frankfort; Nachmais, David. 2008. Research methods in the Social Sciences: Seventh Edition New York, NY: Worth Publishers

focus troupe

WHAT IS IT?

The design team and users act out dramatic vignettes following scripts demonstrating a new product, service or experience. The play presents the problems, and expectations of the design. If actors have some experience of the product or service they can use this.

WHO INVENTED IT?

Sato and Salvador 1999

WHY USE THIS METHOD?

1. You are likely to find new possibilities and problems.
2. Generates empathy for users.
3. This method is an experiential design tool. Bodystorming helps design ideation by exploring context.
4. It is fast and inexpensive.
5. It is a form of physical prototyping
6. It is difficult to imagine misuse scenarios

CHALLENGES

1. Works best with a physical prototype of design.
2. Time is required to write scripts.
3. Some team members may find acting a difficult task.

WHEN TO USE THIS METHOD

1. Know Context
2. Know User
3. Frame insights

HOW TO USE THIS METHOD

1. Select team.
2. Define the locations where a design will be used.
3. Go to those locations and observe how people interact. the artifacts in their environment.
4. Develop the prototypes and props that you need to explore an idea. Identify the people, personas and scenarios that may help you with insight into the design directions.
5. Write scripts
6. Bodystorm the scenarios.
7. Record the scenarios with video and analyze them for insights.

RESOURCES

1. Empathy tools
2. A large room
3. White board
4. Video camera

REFERENCES

1. Understanding Your Users: A Practical Guide to User Requirements Methods By Catherine Courage, Kathy Baxter, Catherine Courage

idiographic approach

WHAT IS IT?
This method is an intense study of a person emphasizing that person's uniqueness. This differs from research that concentrates on common or repeated forms of behavior

WHO INVENTED IT?
Piaget 1953

WHY USE THIS METHOD?
1. May provide a more in depth understanding of an individual.

CHALLENGES
1. Difficult to generalize findings
2. Freud and Paiget created universal theories on the basis of unrepresentative individuals.

WHEN TO USE THIS METHOD
1. Know Context
2. Know User
3. Frame insights

HOW TO USE THIS METHOD
1. Use case studies
2. Use flexible long term procedures.

RESOURCES
1. Video camera
2. Camera
3. Digital voice recorder
4. Note pad
5. Pens

REFERENCES
1. Cone, J. D. (1986). Idiographic, nomothetic, and related perspectives in behavioral assessment. In R. O. Nelson & S. C. Hayes (Eds.): Conceptual foundations of behavioral assessment (pp. 111—128). New York: Guilford.

innovation diagnostic

WHAT IS IT?

An innovation diagnostic is an evaluation of an organization's innovation capabilities. It reviews practices by stakeholders which may help or hinder innovation. An innovation diagnostic is the first step in preparing an implementing a strategy to create an organizational culture that supports innovation.

WHY USE THIS METHOD?

1. It helps organizations develop sustainable competitive advantage.
2. Helps identify innovation opportunities
3. Helps develop innovation strategy.

WHEN TO USE THIS METHOD

1. Know Context
2. Know User
3. Frame insights
4. Explore Concepts
5. Make Plans

HOW TO USE THIS METHOD

An innovation diagnostic reviews organizational and stakeholder practices using both qualitative and quantitative methods including

1. The design and development process
2. Strategic practices and planning.
3. The ability of an organization to monitor and respond to relevant trends.
4. Technologies
5. Organizational flexibility
6. Ability to innovate repeatedly and consistently

interview: naturalistic group

WHAT IS IT?

Naturalistic group interview is an interview method where the participants know each other prior to the interview and so have conversations that are more natural than participants who do not know each other.

WHY USE THIS METHOD?

1. This method has been applied in research in Asia where beliefs are informed by group interaction.
2. Can help gain useful data in cultures where people are less willing to share their feelings.

CHALLENGES

1. Familiarity of participants can lead to groupthink.

WHEN TO USE THIS METHOD

2. Know Context
3. Know User

HOW TO USE THIS METHOD

1. The interview context should support natural conversation.
2. Select participants who have existing social relationships.
3. Group the participants in natural ways so that the conversation is as close as possible to the type of discussion they would have in their everyday life.
4. Groups should be no larger than four people for best results.

RESOURCES

1. Video camera
2. Note pad
3. Pens
4. Use local moderator

REFERENCES

1. Bengtsson, Anders, and Giana M. Eckhardt. "Naturalistic Group Interviewing in China." Qualitative Market Research: An International Journal. 12:1 (2010): 36–44.

interviews: photo elicitation

WHAT IS IT?
Photos are used by a researcher as a focus to discuss the experiences, thoughts and feelings of participants.

WHY USE THIS METHOD?
1. A method sometimes used to interview children.
2. Photos can make staring a conversation with a participant easier.
3. Photos can uncover meaning which is not uncovered in a face to face interview.

CHALLENGES
1. Photos can create ethical questions for the researcher.
2. A researcher may show bias in selecting subject of photos.

RESOURCES
1. Note pad
2. Pens
3. Camera
4. Video camera
5. Digital voice recorder

WHEN TO USE THIS METHOD
1. Know Context
2. Know User

HOW TO USE THIS METHOD
1. Define the context.
2. Select the participants
3. Either researcher or participant may take the photos.
4. Researcher analyses photos and plans the interview process
5. Researcher shows the photos to the participant and discusses their thoughts in relation to the photographs.
6. The interview is analyzed by the researcher.
7. The researcher creates a list of insights.

REFERENCES
1. M. Clark-Ibáñez. Framing the social world with photo-elicitation interviews. American Behavioral Scientist,47(12):1507--1527, 2004.

method bank

WHAT IS IT?

A Method Bank is a central bank where design methods are documented by an organization's employees and can be accessed and applied by other employees.

WHO INVENTED IT?

1. Lego have compiled a Design Practice and emerging methods bank. Microsoft have a methods bank in their Online User Experience best practice intranet.
2. Starbucks have a methods bank in their online workflow management tool

WHY USE THIS METHOD?

1. This approaches helps document tacit knowledge within an organization.

WHEN TO USE THIS METHOD

1. Define intent
2. Know Context
3. Know User
4. Frame insights
5. Explore Concepts
6. Make Plans
7. Deliver Offering

HOW TO USE THIS METHOD

1. Methods are uploaded to the intranet bank.
2. The bank may include descriptions, video, images charts or sketches.

RESOURCES

1. Intranet
2. Camera
3. Video camera
4. Templates
5. Data base.
6. Computers

nomothetic approach

WHAT IS IT?
Nomothetic approach is the approach of investigating a large group of people to find general laws of behavior that apply to everybody. The term "nomothetic" comes from the Greek word "nomos" meaning "law"

WHO INVENTED IT?
Wilhelm Windelband (1848–1915), M.T. Conner 1986, R.P.J. Freeman 1993 and O. Sharpe 2005

WHY USE THIS METHOD?
1. Useful for designing mass produced products or services.

CHALLENGES
1. Individuals are unique.
2. Superficial understanding of any single person.

WHEN TO USE THIS METHOD
1. Define intent
2. Know Context
3. Know User
4. Frame insights

REFERENCES
1. Butterworth-Heinemann, Elsevior (2005). Research Methods. British Library: Elsevior Ltd. pp. 32.
2. Cone, J. D. (1986). Idiographic, nomothetic, and related perspectives in behavioral assessment. In R. O. Nelson & S. C. Hayes (Eds.): Conceptual foundations of behavioral assessment (pp. 111–128). New York: Guilford.
3. Thomae, H. (1999). The nomothetic-idiographic issue: Some roots and recent trends. International Journal of Group Tensions, 28(1), 187–215.

hawthorne effect

WHAT IS IT?
The Hawthorne effect is a psychological theory that the behavior of a person or a group of people will change if they know that they are being observed.

WHO INVENTED IT?
First documented by a research team led by Elton Mayo between 1924 and 1932 at the Western Electric Company Hawthorne plant in Cicero, Illinois. The term was first used by Elton Mayo and Fritz Roethlisberger around 1950.

WHY USE THIS METHOD?
1. Researchers should be aware of the effect to obtain valid results.

CHALLENGES
1. Various writers believe that the original observations and conclusions were overstated including Steven Levitt, John A. List, Adair and H. McIlvaine Parsons

WHEN TO USE THIS METHOD
1. Know Context
2. Know User
3. Frame insights

HOW TO USE THIS METHOD
1. If you conduct a taste test of two beverages and tell the participants who makes the beverages before the test it may influence which beverage that the participants say they prefer.
2. It you tell some participants that they are taking an appetite suppressant then they may eat less even if they are not taking an appetite suppressant.

REFERENCES
1. French, John R. P., "Experiments in Field Settings," in Leon Festinger and Daniel Katz(Eds.), Research Methods in the Behavorial Sciences, Dryden Press, 1953, p. 101.
2. Levitt, Steven D. & List, John A. (2011). "Was There Really a Hawthorne Effect at the Hawthorne Plant? An Analysis of the Original Illumination Experiments". American Economic Journal: Applied Economics 3 (1): 224—238.

object stimulation

WHAT IS IT?

Object stimulation is an idea-generation technique that stimulates different perspectives and ideas.

WHO INVENTED IT?

Clark & Sugrue, 1988

WHY USE THIS METHOD?

1. "According to Gar eld et al. [1997], McFadzean [1996], and Nagasundaram and Bostrom [1993], groups utilizing paradigm-stretching and paradigm-breaking techniques produce more creative ideas "

Source: Elspeth McFadzean

CHALLENGES

1. This technique requires imagination

RESOURCES

1. White board or flip chart
2. Dry erase markers
3. Paper
4. Pens
5. Video camera

REFERENCES

1. McFanzean, E. (1998) The creativity continuum toward a classification of creative problem solving techniques, Creativity and Innovation Management, Vol. 7, No 3, pp. 131-139

WHEN TO USE THIS METHOD

1. Explore Concepts

HOW TO USE THIS METHOD

1. "Write the problem statement on a flip chart.
2. Ask the group members to list objects that are completely unrelated to the problem.
3. Ask one individual to select an object and describe it in detail. The group should use this descriptions a stimulus to generate new and novel ideas.
4. Write each idea on a flip chart.
5. Continue the process until each group member has described an object or until all the objects have been described.
6. Ask the participants to relate the ideas back to the problem and to develop them into practical solutions."

Source: Elspeth McFadzean

observation: covert

WHAT IS IT?

Covert observation is to observe people without them knowing. The identity of the researcher and the purpose of the research are hidden from the people being observed.

WHY USE THIS METHOD?

1. This method may be used to reduce the effect of the observer's presence on the behavior of the subjects.
2. To capture behavior as it happens.
3. Researcher is more likely to observe natural behavior

CHALLENGES

1. The method raises serious ethical questions.
2. Observation does not explain the cause of behavior.
3. Can be difficult to gain access and maintain cover
4. Analysis can be time consuming.
5. Observer bias can cause the researcher to look only where they think they will see useful information.

RESOURCES

1. Camera
2. Video Camera
3. Digital voice recorder

WHEN TO USE THIS METHOD

1. Know Context
2. Know User

HOW TO USE THIS METHOD

1. Define objectives.
2. Define participants and obtain their cooperation.
3. Define The context of the observation: time and place.
4. In some countries the law requires that you obtain written consent to video people.
5. Define the method of observation and the method of recording information. Common methods are taking written notes, video or audio recording.
6. Run a test session.
7. Hypothesize an explanation for the phenomenon.
8. Predict a logical consequence of the hypothesis.
9. Test your hypothesis by observation
10. Analyze the data gathered and create a list of insights derived from the observations.

REFERENCES

1. Ethical Challenges in Participant Observation: A Reflection on Ethnographic Fieldwork By Li, Jun Academic journal article from The Qualitative Report, Vol. 13, No. 1

observation: direct

WHAT IS IT?
Direct Observation is a method in which a re-searcher observes and records behavior events, activities or tasks while something is happening recording observations as they are made.

WHO INVENTED IT?
Radcliff-Brown 1910
Bronisław Malinowski 1922
Margaret Mead 1928

WHY USE THIS METHOD?
1. To capture behavior as it happens.

CHALLENGES
1. Observation does not explain the cause of behavior.
2. Analysis can be time consuming.
3. Observer bias can cause the researcher to look only where they think they will see useful information.
4. Obtain a proper sample for generalization.
5. Observe average workers during average conditions.
6. The participant may change their behavior because they are being watched.

RESOURCES
1. Note pad
2. Pens
3. Camera
4. Video Camera
5. Digital voice recorder

WHEN TO USE THIS METHOD
6. Know Context
7. Know User

HOW TO USE THIS METHOD
1. Define objectives.
2. Make direct observation plan
3. Define participants and obtain their cooperation.
4. Define The context of the observation: time and place.
5. In some countries the law requires that you obtain written consent to video people.
6. Define the method of observation and the method of recording information. Common methods are taking written notes, video or audio recording.
7. Run a test session.
8. Hypothesize an explanation for the phenomenon.
9. Predict a logical consequence of the hypothesis.
10. Test your hypothesis by observation
11. Analyze the data gathered and create a list of insights derived from the observations.

REFERENCES
1. Zechmeister, John J. Shaughnessy, Eugene B. Zechmeister, Jeanne S. (2009). Research methods in psychology (8th ed. ed.). Boston [etc.]: McGraw-Hill. ISBN 9780071283519.

observation: indirect

WHAT IS IT?

This is a method where the observer is unobtrusive and is sometimes used for sensitive research subjects.

WHY USE THIS METHOD?

1. To capture behavior as it happens in it's natural setting.
2. Indirect observation uncovers activity that may have previously gone unnoticed
3. May be inexpensive
4. Can collect a wide range of data

CHALLENGES

1. Observation does not explain the cause of behavior.
2. Analysis can be time consuming.
3. Observer bias can cause the researcher to look only where they think they will see useful information.
4. Obtain a proper sample for generalization.
5. Observe average workers during average conditions.
6. The participant may change their behavior because they are being watched.

WHEN TO USE THIS METHOD

1. Know Context
2. Know User

HOW TO USE THIS METHOD

3. Determine research goals.

RESOURCES

1. Note pad
2. Pens
3. Camera
4. Video Camera
5. Digital voice recorder

REFERENCES

1. Friedman, M. P., & Wilson, R. W. (1975). Application of unobtrusive measures to the study of textbook usage by college students. Journal of Applied Psychology, 60, 659 – 662.
2. Zechmeister, John J. Shaughnessy, Eugene B. Zechmeister, Jeanne S. (2009). Research methods in psychology (8th ed. ed.). Boston [etc.]: McGraw-Hill. ISBN 9780071283519.

observation: non participant

WHAT IS IT?
The observer does not become part of the situation being observed or intervene in the behavior of the subjects. Used when a researcher wants the participants to behave normally. Usually this type of observation occurs in places where people normally work or live

WHY USE THIS METHOD?
1. To capture behavior as it happens.

CHALLENGES
1. Observation does not explain the cause of behavior.
2. Analysis can be time consuming.
3. Observer bias can cause the researcher to look only where they think they will see useful information.
4. Obtain a proper sample for generalization.
5. Observe average workers during average conditions.
6. The participant may change their behavior because they are being watched.

WHEN TO USE THIS METHOD
1. Know Context
2. Know User

HOW TO USE THIS METHOD
1. Determine research goals.
2. Select a research context
3. The site should allow clear observation and be accessible.
4. Select participants
5. Seek permission.
6. Gain access
7. Gather research data.
8. Analyze data
9. Find common themes
10. Create insights

RESOURCES
1. Note pad
2. Pens
3. Camera
4. Video Camera
5. Digital voice recorder

REFERENCES
1. Zechmeister, John J. Shaughnessy, Eugene B. Zechmeister, Jeanne S. (2009). Research methods in psychology (8th ed. ed.). Boston [etc.]: McGraw-Hill. ISBN 9780071283519.

observation: participant

WHAT IS IT?

Participant observation is an observation method where the researcher participates. The researcher becomes part of the situation being studied. The researcher may live or work in the context of the participant and may become an accepted member of the participant's community. This method was used extensively by the pioneers of field research.

WHO INVENTED IT?

Radcliff-Brown 1910
Bronisław Malinowski 1922
Margaret Mead 1928

WHY USE THIS METHOD?

1. The goal of this method is to become close and familiar with the behavior of the participants.
2. To capture behavior as it happens.

CHALLENGES

1. My be time consuming
2. May be costly
3. The researcher may influence the behavior of the participants.
4. The participants may not show the same behavior if the observer was not present.
5. May be language barriers
6. May be cultural barriers
7. May be risks for the researcher.
8. Be open to possibilities.
9. Be sensitive to privacy, and confidentiality.

WHEN TO USE THIS METHOD

1. Know Context
2. Know User

HOW TO USE THIS METHOD

1. Determine research goals.
2. Select a research context
3. The site should allow clear observation and be accessible.
4. Select participants
5. Seek permission.
6. Gain access
7. Gather research data.
8. Analyze data
9. Find common themes
10. Create insights

RESOURCES

1. Note pad
2. Pens
3. Camera
4. Video Camera
5. Digital voice recorder

REFERENCES

1. Malinowski, Bronisław (1929) The sexual life of savages in north-western Melanesia: an ethnographic account of courtship, marriage and family life among the natives of the Trobriand Islands, British New Guinea. New York: Halcyon House.
2. Marek M. Kaminski. 2004. Games Prisoners Play. Princeton University Press. ISBN 0-691-11721-7

observation: overt

WHAT IS IT?
A method of observation where the subjects are aware that they are being observed

WHO INVENTED IT?
Radcliff-Brown 1910
Bronisław Malinowski 1922
Margaret Mead 1928

WHY USE THIS METHOD?
1. To capture behavior as it happens.

CHALLENGES
1. Observation does not explain the cause of behavior.
2. Analysis can be time consuming.
3. Observer bias can cause the researcher to look only where they think they will see useful information.

RESOURCES
1. Note pad
2. Pens
3. Camera
4. Video Camera
5. Digital voice recorder

REFERENCES
1. Zechmeister, John J. Shaughnessy, Eugene B. Zechmeister, Jeanne S. (2009). Research methods in psychology (8th ed. ed.). Boston [etc.]: McGraw-Hill. ISBN 9780071283519.

WHEN TO USE THIS METHOD
1. Know Context
2. Know User

HOW TO USE THIS METHOD
1. Define objectives.
2. Define participants and obtain their cooperation.
3. Define The context of the observation: time and place.
4. In some countries the law requires that you obtain written consent to video people.
5. Define the method of observation and the method of recording information. Common methods are taking written notes, video or audio recording.
6. Run a test session.
7. Hypothesize an explanation for the phenomenon.
8. Predict a logical consequence of the hypothesis.
9. Test your hypothesis by observation
10. Analyze the data gathered and create a list of insights derived from the observations.

observation: structured

WHAT IS IT?

Particular types of behavior are observed and counted like a survey. The observer may create an event so that the behavior can be more easily studied. This approach is systematically planned and executed.

WHY USE THIS METHOD?

1. Allows stronger generalizations than unstructured observation.
2. May allow an observer to study behavior that may be difficult to study in unstructured observation.
3. To capture behavior as it happens.
4. A procedure is used which can be replicated.

CHALLENGES

1. Observation does not explain the cause of behavior.
2. Analysis can be time consuming.
3. Observer bias can cause the researcher to look only where they think they will see useful information.

RESOURCES

1. Note pad
2. Pens
3. Camera
4. Video Camera
5. Digital voice recorder

WHEN TO USE THIS METHOD

1. Know Context
2. Know User

HOW TO USE THIS METHOD

1. Define objectives.
2. Define participants and obtain their cooperation.
3. Define The context of the observation: time and place.
4. In some countries the law requires that you obtain written consent to video people.
5. Define the method of observation and the method of recording information. Common methods are taking written notes, video or audio recording.
6. Run a test session.
7. Hypothesize an explanation for the phenomenon.
8. Predict a logical consequence of the hypothesis.
9. Test your hypothesis by observation
10. Analyze the data gathered and create a list of insights derived from the observations.

REFERENCES

1. Zechmeister, John J. Shaughnessy, Eugene B. Zechmeister, Jeanne S. (2009). Research methods in psychology (8th ed. ed.). Boston [etc.]: McGraw-Hill. ISBN 9780071283519.

observation: unstructured

WHAT IS IT?

This method is used when a researcher wants to see what is naturally occurring without predetermined ideas. We use have an open-ended approach to observation and record all that we observe

WHY USE THIS METHOD?

1. To capture behavior as it happens.
2. This form of observation is appropriate when the problem has yet to be formulated precisely and flexibility is needed in observation to identify key components of the problem and to develop hypotheses
3. Observation is the most direct measure of behavior

CHALLENGES

1. Replication may be difficult.
2. Observation does not explain the cause of behavior.
3. Analysis can be time consuming.
4. Observer bias can cause the researcher to look only where they think they will see useful information.
5. Data cannot be quantified
6. In this form of observation there is a higher probability of observer's bias.

WHEN TO USE THIS METHOD

1. Know Context
2. Know User

HOW TO USE THIS METHOD

1. Select a context to explore
2. Take a camera, note pad and pen
3. Record things and questions that you find interesting
4. Record ideas as you form them
5. Do not reach conclusions.
6. Ask people questions and try to understand the meaning in their replies.

RESOURCES

1. Note pad
2. Pens
3. Camera
4. Video Camera
5. Digital voice recorder

REFERENCES

1. Zechmeister, John J. Shaughnessy, Eugene B. Zechmeister, Jeanne S. (2009). Research methods in psychology (8th ed. ed.). Boston [etc.]: McGraw-Hill. ISBN 9780071283519.

online methods

WHAT IS IT?

Online testing is a method of obtaining feedback for a design relatively quickly and cost effectively. It is an emerging area of design research.

Some areas are:

1. Online ethnography
2. Online focus groups
3. Online interviews
4. Online questionnaires
5. Web-based experiments
6. Online clinical trials

WHY USE THIS METHOD?

1. You can reach a large number of people
2. Flexible
3. Time and cost effective
4. New media seem to offer the hope of reaching different populations of research subjects in new ways
5. Access to populations
6. May be more acceptable method for participants.

CHALLENGES

1. May not be the fastest method of getting feedback.
2. Participants may lose interest quickly.
3. High drop out rates.
4. Participant's input from senses is limited to vision
5. Is a method that is still being adopted.
6. Sensitivity is required in internet research for legal, practical and ethical reasons.

WHEN TO USE THIS METHOD

1. Know Context
2. Know User

HOW TO USE THIS METHOD

This is a complex and growing area of research. Some guidelines are

1. E-mail can be used for online focus groups using the copy all function.
2. Because participants can reply at any time moderation may be more difficult than a face to face focus group.
3. Group interaction may be less than in a face to face interview or focus group.
4. Social networks can be useful in generating lively discussions and allowing interaction within the social context of a group

RESOURCES

1. Computer
2. Text editor
3. Internet connection
4. Social network connections

REFERENCES

1. Fischer, M., Lyon, S. and Zeitlyn, D. (2008) The internet and the future of social science research. In Fielding, N., Lee, R. M. and Blank, G. (Eds.), The SAGE handbook of Online Research Methods. London. SAGE. pp. 519–536.
2. Hewson, C., Yule, P., Laurent, D. and Vogel, C. (2003) Internet Research Methods. London. Sage.

online methods: ethnography

WHAT IS IT?

Online ethnography refers to a number of related online research methods that adapt ethnographic methods to the study of the communities and cultures created through computer-mediated social interaction

WHO INVENTED IT?

One of the early published articles identifying emerging online ethnography was by Arnould and Wallendorf 1994

WHY USE THIS METHOD?

1. New level of access to people
2. Access to more people
3. Easier access than traditional ethnography
4. Less expensive Than traditional ethnography.
5. Faster than traditional methods

CHALLENGES

1. Some believe that new methods need to be developed that are distinctively different than face to face ethnographic methods.

WHEN TO USE THIS METHOD

1. Know Context
2. Know User

HOW TO USE THIS METHOD

There are diverse methods developing for ethnographic study via the internet.

1. Netnography
2. Online Interviews
3. Online focus groups
4. Online Communities and Cultures

RESOURCES

1. Computer
2. Web browser
3. Internet connection

REFERENCES

1. Wilson, Samuel M.; Peterson, Leighton C. (2002). "The Anthropology of Online Communities". Annual Review of Anthropology 31: 449–467.
2. Domínguez, Daniel; Beaulieu, Anne; Estalella, Adolfo; Gómez, Edgar; Schnettler, Bernt & Read, Rosie (2007). Virtual Ethnography. Forum Qualitative Sozialforschung / Forum: Qualitative Social Research, 8(3), http://nbn-resolving.de/urn:nbn:de:0114-fqs0703E19.

online methods: clinical trials

WHAT IS IT?

An online clinical trail involves the use of the internet to conduct a clinical trial in part or in whole.

US National Cancer Institute and the University of California, San Francisco, School of Medicine maintain websites with suggested methods and templates for phase I — III studies. Because of the complexity and critical nature of this method the author suggests that you review those site for more information. [2] [3]

WHO INVENTED IT?

In 2011, the US FDA approved a Phase 1 trial that used remote patient monitoring, to collect data in patients' homes and transmit it electronically to the trial database.

WHY USE THIS METHOD?

1. Using Internet resources may reduce the expense and development time of a clinical trial.
2. The processes of patient registration, randomization, data collection, analysis, and publication can all be accomplished with online resources

CHALLENGES

1. Security is a central issue when considering the Internet for sensitive information exchange

WHEN TO USE THIS METHOD

1. Know Context
2. Know User

REFERENCES

1. The Internet and Clinical Trials: Background, Online Resources, Examples and Issues. James Paul; Rachael Seib; Todd Prescott. Journal of Medical Internet Research Vol 7 (1) 2005
2. US National Cancer Institute, Cancer Therapy Evaluation Program, authors. Protocol templates, applications and guidelines. 2004. [2004 Aug 16]. http://ctep.cancer.gov/guidelines/templates.html.
3. University of California, San Francisco, School of Medicine, authors. UCSF clinical research manuals and guidelines. 2004. [2004 Aug 16]. http://medschool.ucsf.edu/research_forms/

online methods: focus groups

WHAT IS IT?
An online focus group is a focus group conducted via the internet. It is one of a number of online research methods.

WHO INVENTED IT?
Greenfield Online, Inc. Filed a patent on January 22, 1999 for 'System and Method For Conducting Focus Groups Using Remotely Located Participants Over A Computer Network.'

WHY USE THIS METHOD?
1. Consumer research
2. Political research
3. Business to business research.
4. Less expensive and faster to organize than face to face focus groups.
5. Avoids travel expenses.
6. Greater geographic reach.

CHALLENGES
1. Body language less readable

WHEN TO USE THIS METHOD
1. Know Context
2. Know User

HOW TO USE THIS METHOD
1. Invite pre screened qualified subjects who represent the target to participate.
2. Define incentives
3. Prepare questions.
4. Usually usually limited to 8–10 participants.
5. Durations is generally one hour to 90 minutes
6. Can record via web cams participants face while they undertake exercises.
7. Use software that facilitates White board style exercises that are visible to participants.
8. Respondents should interact with each other and with the moderator.

RESOURCES
1. Online focus group interface
2. Computer
3. Web browser
4. Internet connection.

online methods: interviews

WHAT IS IT?
With this method an interview is conducted via internet.

WHY USE THIS METHOD?
1. Possible to access a geographically dispersed population;
2. Possible savings in costs to the researcher
3. Reduce issues of interviewer effect as participants cannot 'see' each other

CHALLENGES
1. Lack of communication of body language.
2. Establishing a good rapport may be more difficult.
3. Higher drop out rate.
4. Lack of visibility of distractions.

RESOURCES
1. Computer
2. Internet connection
3. Notebook
4. Pens
5. Interview plan or structure
6. Questions, tasks and discussion items
7. Confidentiality agreement

WHEN TO USE THIS METHOD
1. Know Context
2. Know User

HOW TO USE THIS METHOD
Technologies include news groups and forums and e-mail.
1. Choose a topic
2. Identify a subject.
3. Contact subject and obtain approval.
4. An asynchronous online interview is one where the researcher and the researched are not necessarily online at the same time.
5. Prepare interview questions.
6. Conduct interview
7. Analyze data.

REFERENCES
1. Mann and Stewart (2005) Internet Communication and Qualitative Research: A Handbook for Researching Online London: Sage

online methods: questionnaires

WHAT IS IT?
An online questionnaire is a questionnaire conducted via the internet.

WHY USE THIS METHOD?
1. Web surveys are faster, simpler and cheaper
2. Data collection period is significantly shortened
3. Simple to compile data
4. Complex skip patterns can be implemented in ways that are mostly invisible to the respondent
5. According to ESOMAR online survey research accounted for 20% of global data-collection expenditure in 2006.

CHALLENGES
1. Response rates are generally low
2. Sample selection bias that is out of research control

REFERENCES
1. Burns, A. C., & Bush, R. F. (2010). Marketing Research. Upper Saddle River, NJ: Pearson Education.
2. Foddy, W. H. (1994). Constructing questions for interviews and questionnaires: Theory and practice in social research (New ed.). Cambridge, UK: Cambridge University Press.

WHEN TO USE THIS METHOD
1. Know Context
2. Know User

HOW TO USE THIS METHOD
1. It is recommended that the time taken to complete an online questionnaire should not exceed 5 minutes.
2. Pretest the questionnaire with at least 5 people, prior to publication on the web.
3. The questionnaire should begin with a short introduction that explains to the participant why it is being conducted and what the information will be used for.
4. Use "smart branching" to lessen complexity. Jump to the next relevant question based on a particular answer.
5. Include a "Thank you" statement at the end.
6. Use statements which are interpreted in the same way by different cultures.
7. Use statements where people that have different opinions will give different answers.
8. Use positive statements and avoid negatives or double negatives.
9. Do not make assumptions about the respondent.
10. Use clear and comprehensible wording, easily understandable for all educational levels
11. Avoid items that contain more than one question per item

online methods: experiments

WHAT IS IT?
A internet based experiment is an experiment that is conducted over the Internet.

WHO INVENTED IT?
Early study by Reips and Bosnjak, 2001

WHY USE THIS METHOD?
1. Researchers can collect large amounts of research material from a wide range of locations and people at relatively low expense.

CHALLENGES
1. Web-based experiments may have weaker experimental controls

WHEN TO USE THIS METHOD
1. Know Context
2. Know User

HOW TO USE THIS METHOD
1. Consider using a web-based software tool
2. Pretest your experiment for clarity of instructions and availability on different platforms.
3. Check your Web experiment for configuration errors
4. Run your experiment both online and offline,for comparison.
5. Ask filter questions
6. Check for obvious naming of files,conditions,and,if applicable,passwords.
7. Perform consistency checks.
8. Report and analyze dropout curves
Source [1]

online methods: online ethics

HOW TO USE THIS METHOD
Below are some guidelines for online research.

1. Participant should not be obliged to answer questions
2. Incentives to take a survey should be used as little as possible.
3. Questionnaires should allow respondents to remain anonymous.
4. Sensitive questionnaires should be confidential.
5. Questions should have the option of "I don't know" or an option that denotes neutrality
6. Questions should not trick the participant.
7. Participant should know why the questionnaire is taking place
8. Participant should know what the information will be used for.
9. In sensitive cases, the questionnaire should be reviewed by an ethics committee or outside party.

REFERENCES

1. Reips, Ulf-Dietrich . (2007). The methodology of Internet-based experiments. In A. Joinson, K. McKenna, T. Postmes, & U.-D. Reips (Eds.), The Oxford Handbook of Internet Psychology (pp. 373-390). Oxford: Oxford University Press.
1. Reips Ulf-Dietrich Standards for Internet-Based Experimenting Experimental and Developmental Psychology, 2002 University of Zürich, Switzerland
2. Reips, U.-D. (2002). Standards for Internet-based experimenting. Experimental Psychology, 49 (4), 243-256.

open ended questions

WHAT IS IT?

Open ended questions are questions that encourage a broad meaningful responses from a respondent rather than a simple yes or no answer.

WHY USE THIS METHOD?

1. Are more objective than close ended questions
2. Better than close ended questions when probing sensitive topics with respondents.
3. Good method in focus groups.

CHALLENGES

1. Should be combined with close ended questions.
2. Perceived as less threatening than open close ended questions.
3. Take more time than close ended questions

WHEN TO USE THIS METHOD

1. Know Context
2. Know User

HOW TO USE THIS METHOD

1. Ask close ended question first if respondents are not comfortable talking.
2. Follow-up with "Why?" or "How?"
3. Ask questions that encourage people to talk.
4. An example of an open ended question may be "Why did it happen?" or "What happened then?"
5. Try to listen to the answer

RESOURCES

1. Pen
2. Paper
3. Video camera
4. Digital voice recorder
5. Question guide

REFERENCES

1. Howard Schuman and Stanley Presser (October 1979). "The Open and Closed Question". American Sociological Review 44 (5): 692–712.

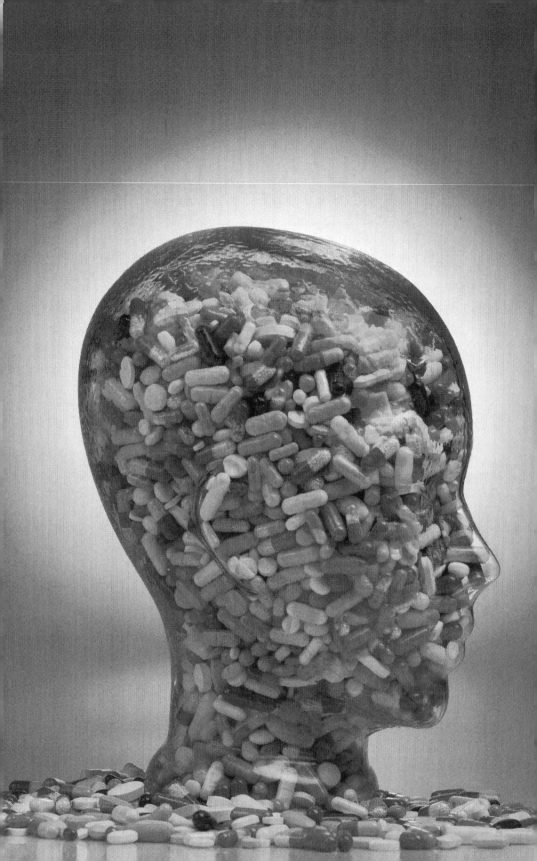

placebo controlled study

WHAT IS IT?
A Placebo-controlled study is a study where a group of subjects receives a treatment and a second group receives a similar treatment that is designed to have no effect.

WHO INVENTED IT?
James Lind 1747

WHY USE THIS METHOD?
1. The purpose of this method is to understand the effects of treatment that do not depend on the treatment itself.

CHALLENGES
1. Ethical questions regarding disclosure
2. Ethical questions regarding the relationship of research and treatment.

WHEN TO USE THIS METHOD
1. Know Context
2. Know User
3. Frame insights

HOW TO USE THIS METHOD
Three groups of participants are created:
1. The group for active treatment
2. The group to receive placebo treatment
3. The group to receive no treatment.

The treatment and placebo treatment are given
The outcomes are observed and compared

REFERENCES
1. Harman WW, McKim RH, Mogar RE, Fadiman J, Stolaroff MJ (August 1966). "Psychedelic agents in creative problem-solving: a pilot study". Psychol Rep 19 (1): 211–27. PMID 5942087.
2. Lasagna L, Mosteller F, von Felsinger JM, Beecher HK (June 1954). "A study of the placebo response". Am. J. Med. 16 (6): 770–9. doi:10.1016/0002-9343(54)90441-6. PMID 13158365.

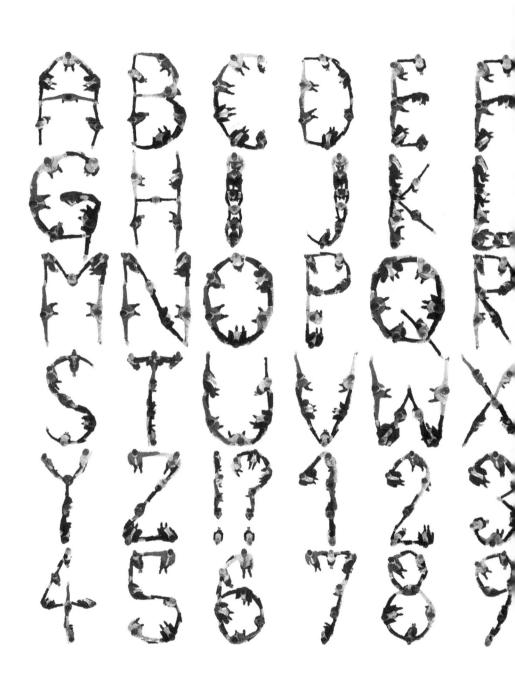

221

sampling: cluster

WHAT IS IT?

This sampling method is often used to save time and cost when a population is widely dispersed. Dividing a geographic area into clusters is a first step. Following this step, clusters are then sampled.

WHY USE THIS METHOD?

1. May reduce the average cost per interview.

CHALLENGES

1. Higher sampling error than some other methods.

WHEN TO USE THIS METHOD

2. Know Context
3. Know User
4. Frame insights

HOW TO USE THIS METHOD

1. Define the population to be sampled.
2. Divide the population into groups or clusters.
3. Determine the sample size.
4. Select a representative sample from the targeted population.
5. Collect the data from each group.
6. Analyze the data

REFERENCES

1. Kerry and Bland (1998). Statistics notes: The intracluster correlation coefficient in cluster randomisation. British Medical Journal, 316, 1455–1460.
2. Babbie, E. (2001). The Practice of Social Research: 9th Edition. Belmont, CA: Wadsworth Thomson.

sampling: convenience

WHAT IS IT?

A sampling method that uses people who are easily available to sample. Convenience sampling is also known as Opportunity Sampling, Accidental Sampling or Haphazard Sampling.

WHO INVENTED IT?

Pierre Simon Laplace pioneered sampling 1786

WHY USE THIS METHOD?

1. Use when time is limited
2. Use when budgets are limited

CHALLENGES

3. Use as many people as possible.

WHEN TO USE THIS METHOD

1. Know Context
2. Know User

HOW TO USE THIS METHOD

1. Use people in the street, friends, work colleagues, customers, fellow students.

REFERENCES

1. Cochran, William G. (1977). Sampling techniques (Third ed.). Wiley. ISBN 0-471-16240-X
2. Robert Groves, et alia. Survey methodology (2010) Second edition of the (2004) first edition ISBN 0-471-48348-6.
3. Chambers, R L, and Skinner, C J (editors) (2003), Analysis of Survey Data, Wiley, ISBN 0-471-89987-9

sampling: random

WHAT IS IT?

With random also called probability sampling, all people in the population being studied have some opportunity of being included in the sample, and the mathematical probability that any one of them will be selected can be calculated.

WHO INVENTED IT?

Pierre Simon Laplace pioneered sampling 1786

WHY USE THIS METHOD?

1. Applicable when population is small, homogeneous & readily available
2. Each person has an equal probability of selection.
3. Estimates are easy to calculate.

CHALLENGES

1. Minority subgroups of interest in population may not be present in sample in sufficient numbers for study.
2. Requires selection of relevant stratification variables which can be difficult.
3. Is not useful when there are no homogeneous subgroups.
4. Can be expensive to implement.

WHEN TO USE THIS METHOD

1. Know Context
2. Know User

HOW TO USE THIS METHOD

1. Define the population to be sampled.
2. Specifying a sampling frame, a set of items or events possible to measure
3. Determine the sample size.
4. Select a representative sample from the targeted population.
5. Implement the sampling plan. A table of random numbers or lottery system is used to determine which are to be selected.
6. Carefully collect required data.

REFERENCES

1. Cochran, William G. (1977). Sampling techniques (Third ed.). Wiley. ISBN 0-471-16240-X
2. Robert Groves, et alia. Survey methodology (2010) Second edition of the (2004) first edition ISBN 0-471-48348-6.
3. Chambers, R L, and Skinner, C J (editors) (2003), Analysis of Survey Data, Wiley, ISBN 0-471-89987-9

sampling: expert

WHAT IS IT?
A method of sampling where experts with a high level of knowledge are sampled.

WHO INVENTED IT?
Pierre Simon Laplace pioneered sampling 1786

WHY USE THIS METHOD?
1. The opinions of experts are respected.
2. May be credible with audience that accepts the people sampled as experts.

CHALLENGES
1. Not everyone will have the same definition of an expert.

WHEN TO USE THIS METHOD
1. Know Context
2. Know User

HOW TO USE THIS METHOD
1. If a pre study define the definition of an expert for the purpose of the sampling process.
2. Select those people who pass the definition of an expert for the sample.

REFERENCES
1. Cochran, William G. (1977). Sampling techniques (Third ed.). Wiley. ISBN 0-471-16240-X
2. Robert Groves, et alia. Survey methodology (2010) Second edition of the (2004) first edition ISBN 0-471-48348-6.
3. Chambers, R L, and Skinner, C J (editors) (2003), Analysis of Survey Data, Wiley, ISBN 0-471-89987-9

sampling: situation

WHAT IS IT?

Situation sampling involves observation of behavior in different locations, circumstances and conditions.

WHO INVENTED IT?

Pierre Simon Laplace pioneered sampling 1786

WHY USE THIS METHOD?

1. Situation sampling enhances the external validity of findings.
2. By sampling behavior in several different situations, you are able to determine whether the behavior in question changes as a function of the context in which you observed it.
3. Your ability to generalize any behavioral consistencies across the various situations is increased.

WHEN TO USE THIS METHOD

1. Know Context
2. Know User

HOW TO USE THIS METHOD

1. When two individuals observe the same behavior, it is possible to see how well their observations agree.

REFERENCES

1. Cochran, William G. (1977). Sampling techniques (Third ed.). Wiley. ISBN 0-471-16240-X
2. Robert Groves, et alia. Survey methodology (2010) Second edition of the (2004) first edition ISBN 0-471-48348-6.
3. Chambers, R L, and Skinner, C J (editors) (2003), Analysis of Survey Data, Wiley, ISBN 0-471-89987-9

sampling: stratified

WHAT IS IT?

A sampling method that addresses the differences of subgroups, called strata, and ensures that a representative percentage is drawn from each stratum to form the sample.

WHO INVENTED IT?

Pierre Simon Laplace pioneered sampling 1786

WHY USE THIS METHOD?

1. Use when there are specific sub-groups to investigate.
2. May achieve greater statistical significance in a smaller sample.
3. May reduce standard error.

WHEN TO USE THIS METHOD

4. Know Context
5. Know User

HOW TO USE THIS METHOD

1. Divide the population up into a set of smaller non-overlapping sub-groups (strata), then do a simple random sample in each sub-group.
2. Strata can be natural groupings, such as age ranges or ethnic origins.

Source: changingminds.org

REFERENCES

1. Cochran, William G. (1977). Sampling techniques (Third ed.). Wiley. ISBN 0-471-16240-X
2. Robert Groves, et alia. Survey methodology (2010) Second edition of the (2004) first edition ISBN 0-471-48348-6.
3. Chambers, R L, and Skinner, C J (editors) (2003), Analysis of Survey Data, Wiley, ISBN 0-471-89987-9

sampling: systematic

WHAT IS IT?

A variation of random sampling in which members of a population are selected at a predetermined interval from a listing, time period, or space. Systematic sampling is also called systematic random sampling. Use when it is easiest to select every nth person.

WHO INVENTED IT?

Pierre Simon Laplace pioneered sampling 1786

WHY USE THIS METHOD?

1. Use when a stream of representative people are available.
2. Use when it is easiest to select every nth person.
3. Use when it is difficult to identify items using a simple random sampling method.

REFERENCES

1. Cochran, William G. (1977). Sampling techniques (Third ed.). Wiley. ISBN 0-471-16240-X
2. Robert Groves, et alia. Survey methodology (2010) Second edition of the (2004) first edition ISBN 0-471-48348-6.
3. Chambers, R L, and Skinner, C J (editors) (2003), Analysis of Survey Data, Wiley, ISBN 0-471-89987-9

WHEN TO USE THIS METHOD

1. Know Context
2. Know User

HOW TO USE THIS METHOD

1. "Identify your sample size, n. Divide the total number of items in the population, N, by n. Round the decimal down. This gives you your interval, k.
2. Thus for a population of 2000 and a sample of 100, k = 2000/100 = 20.
3. Put the population into a sequential order, ensuring the attribute being studied is randomly distributed.
4. Select a random number, x, between 1 and k.
5. The first sampled item is the x-th. Then select every k-th item.
6. Thus if k is 20 and x is 12, select the 12th item, then the 32nd, then the 52nd and so on.
7. In brief: select every nth item, starting with a random one"

Source: changingminds.org

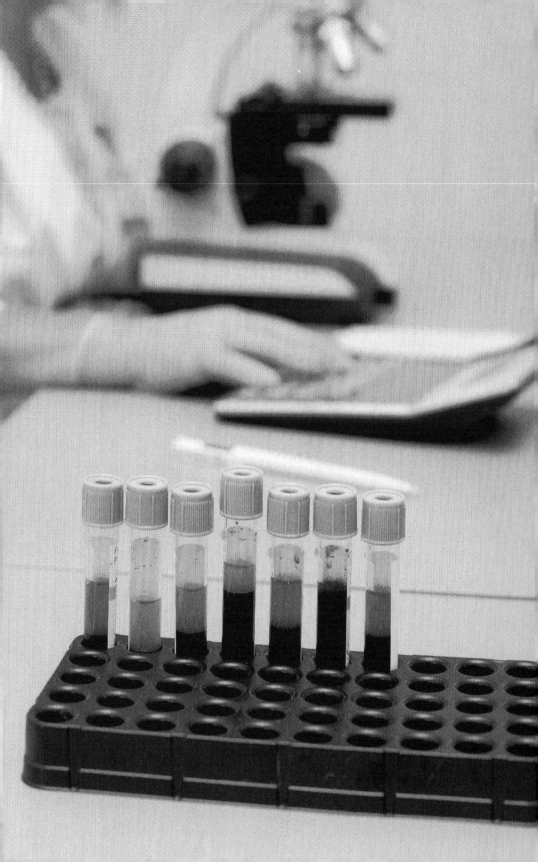

sampling: time

WHAT IS IT?
Researchers choose time intervals for making observations.

WHO INVENTED IT?
Pierre Simon Laplace pioneered sampling 1786

WHY USE THIS METHOD?
The main advantages of sampling are:
1. The cost is lower,
2. Data collection is faster,
3. Time sampling is a useful way to collect and present observation data over a long period of time

CHALLENGES
1. Be careful to record events according to your plan.

WHEN TO USE THIS METHOD
1. Know Context
2. Know User

HOW TO USE THIS METHOD
1. Determine the goal of the research.
2. Select a place and participants.
3. Create a chart to record your data.
4. Carefully collect required data.

REFERENCES
1. Cochran, William G. (1977). Sampling techniques (Third ed.). Wiley. ISBN 0-471-16240-X
2. Robert Groves, et alia. Survey methodology (2010) Second edition of the (2004) first edition ISBN 0-471-48348-6.
3. Chambers, R L, and Skinner, C J (editors) (2003), Analysis of Survey Data, Wiley, ISBN 0-471-89987-9

SOCIOGRAM

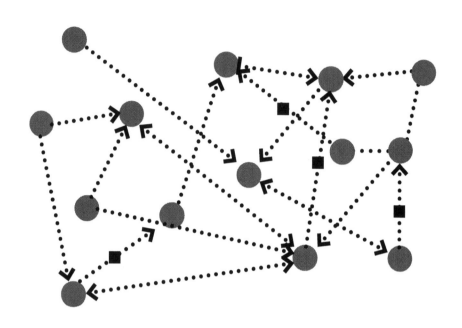

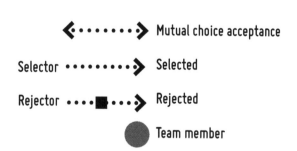

Mutual choice acceptance

Selector ·········> Selected

Rejector ····■···> Rejected

Team member

233

sociogram

WHAT IS IT?

A sociogram is a map of team interactions and structure. It is used to foster partnerships, team cohesiveness and participation.

WHO INVENTED IT?

J. L. Moreno 1934

WHY USE THIS METHOD?

1. A sociogram identifies alliances within the group.

REFERENCES

1. "An Experiential Approach to Organization Development 7th ed."Brown, Donald R.and Harvey, Don. Page 134

WHEN TO USE THIS METHOD

1. Define intent
2. Frame insights
3. Deliver Offering

HOW TO USE THIS METHOD

1. The moderator performs ongoing team observations.
2. Notes are recorded on team observations
3. A sociogram is drawn and shared with the team.
4. An open discussion follows on ways to improve the team's interactions and performance.
5. The team and moderator develop a strategy for improving team performance and interactions.

RESOURCES

1. Paper
2. Pens
3. White board
4. Dry erase markers

Chapter 5
Frame insights
this is what we discovered

BAR CHART

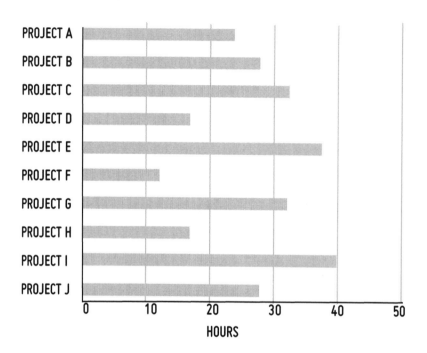

bar chart

WHAT IS IT?

A simple bar chart is useful to present information for a quick problem or opportunity analysis. It provides a comparison of quantities of items or frequencies of events within a particular time period.

WHO INVENTED IT?

The first bar graph appeared in the 1786 book The Commercial and Political Atlas, by William Playfair (1759-1823)

WHY USE THIS METHOD?

1. To display a "snapshot" comparison of categories.
2. To depict the relationship between variations over time.
3. To illustrate process variability or trends.
4. To indicate a potential problem area (high or low frequencies).

CHALLENGES

1. Care should be taken not to insert more than five bars or cover more than five time periods. This would make the Bar Chart cluttered and difficult to interpret.

WHEN TO USE THIS METHOD

1. Frame insights

HOW TO USE THIS METHOD

1. Collect data from sources
2. Draw the vertical and horizontal axes.
3. Decide on the scale
4. Draw a bar for each item.
5. Label the axes

RESOURCES

1. Pen
2. Paper
3. Graph paper
4. Computer
5. Graphics software

REFERENCES

1. Kelley, W. M.; Donnelly, R. A. (2009) The Humongous Book of Statistics Problems. New York, NY: Alpha Books ISBN 1592578659

bullet proofing

WHAT IS IT?
This method is a way of analyzing solutions more vulnerable to threats.

WHO INVENTED IT?
Kepner and Tregoe, Isaksen and Treffinger, 1985

WHY USE THIS METHOD?
1. To identify and plan for possible risks.

REFERENCES
1. J. G. Rawlinson, Creative Thinking and Brainstorming, 1981

RESOURCES
1. Paper
2. Pens
3. White board
4. Dry erase markers

WHEN TO USE THIS METHOD
1. Frame insights
2. Explore Concepts

HOW TO USE THIS METHOD
1. Brainstorm threats that have not yet been identified.
2. Ask
   ◦ "What are the threats?"
   ◦ "What are the greatest threats and how likely are they to occur?"
   ◦ "What's the worst imaginable thing that could occur?"
3. Prioritize the possible threats considering how likely the threat is to occur and how bad the consequences may be if it did occur.
4. Give priority to problem solutions that deal with problems most likely to occur and most serious in their impact.

COMPARATIVE MATRIX

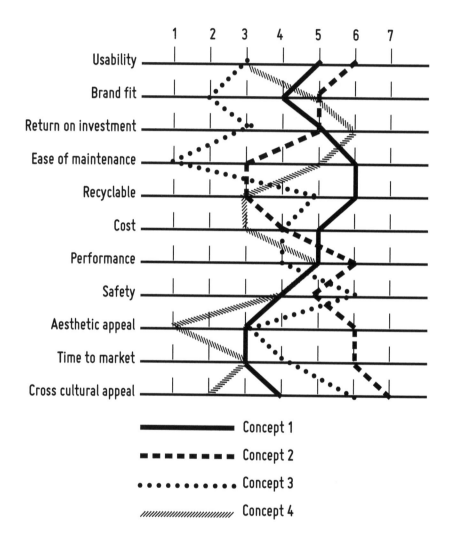

Concept 1
Concept 2
Concept 3
Concept 4

comparative matrix

WHAT IS IT?
A method that can be used to graphically display the responses of a Likert questionnaire.

WHY USE THIS METHOD?
1. An efficient method of comparing responses related to a number of alternatives.

CHALLENGES
1. Use a 7 point scale

WHEN TO USE THIS METHOD
1. Know Context
2. Know User
3. Frame insights

HOW TO USE THIS METHOD
1. Identify data.
1. Create a multiple rating matrix.
2. Collect data
3. Map data.

RESOURCES
1. Pen
2. Paper
3. Computer
4. Graphic software.

delphi method

WHAT IS IT?

The Delphi Method is a forecasting method which relies on a group of experts. The method is widely used in business.

WHO INVENTED IT?

Olaf Helmer, Norman Dalkey, and Nicholas Rescher RAND Corporation 1959

WHY USE THIS METHOD?

1. It is sometimes used to solve poorly defined or difficult problems.
2. It can be a fast method.

WHEN TO USE THIS METHOD

1. Frame insights
2. Explore Concepts
3. Make Plans

CHALLENGES

1. Can be difficult to recruit 15 to 25 experts.
2. Method can be time consuming.
3. Usually the participants remain anonymous.

HOW TO USE THIS METHOD

1. 15 to 25 experts answer questions in two or more sessions of questions
2. After each session a moderator creates a summary of the experts answers with the reasons provided.
3. Experts each generate 15 to 20 concerns.
4. During each session the experts revise their answers based on the views of the other experts.
5. Over a number of sessions the answers converge to a consensus.
6. If consensus is not reach the process continues.

REFERENCES

1. Harold A. Linstone, Murray Turoff (1975), The Delphi Method: Techniques and Applications, Reading, Mass.: Addison-Wesley, ISBN 978-0-201-04294-8
2. Rowe and Wright (2001): Expert Opinions in Forecasting. Role of the Delphi Technique. In: Armstrong (Ed.): Principles of Forecasting: A Handbook of Researchers and Practitioners, Boston: Kluwer Academic Publishers.

DOT DIAGRAM

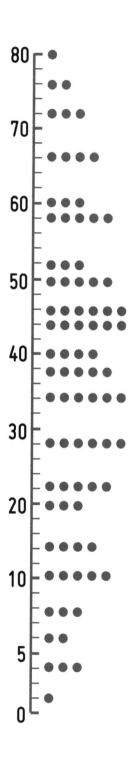

dot diagram

WHAT IS IT?

A dot diagram is a graphic representation of data that shows how often a value occurs. Normal distribution may show a bell shaped curve.

WHY USE THIS METHOD?

1. Used to show the dispersion of data

CHALLENGES

1. A dot diagram should not be used for more than 30 observations.

WHEN TO USE THIS METHOD

2. Frame insights

HOW TO USE THIS METHOD

1. Collect and the data.
2. Sort numbers from low to high. S
3. Draw a horizontal line and mark or scale units of measurement,
4. Place a dot for each number and continue until all numbers have been dotted.
5. The dot diagram displays all values and how often they occurred.

RESOURCES

1. Pen
2. Paper
3. Computer
4. Graphics software

FEATURE PERMUTATION .

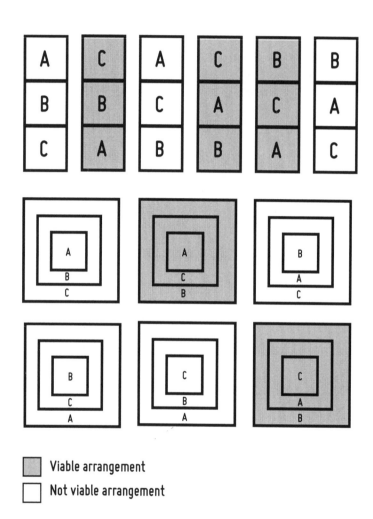

Viable arrangement
Not viable arrangement

feature permutation

WHAT IS IT?
This method rearranges the features of a product in a systematic approach.

WHO INVENTED IT?
Eskild Tjalve

WHY USE THIS METHOD?
1. It is a systematic way of exploring all alternative options of physical relationships of features.

CHALLENGES
1. It may be time consuming to explore every possibility.

RESOURCES
1. Pen
2. Paper
3. White board
4. Dry erase markers

WHEN TO USE THIS METHOD
1. Explore Concepts

HOW TO USE THIS METHOD
1. Define the discreet elements or features of the design'
2. Identify the possible high level arrangements such as linear, partly embedded and embedded.
3. Create simple diagrams that show every feature in every possible arrangement
4. Identify which arrangements may be viable.
5. Explore those arrangements of features in formal 3d concept sketch development.

REFERENCES
1. Baxter, M., Product Design: A practical guide to systematic methods of new product development. London: Chapman & Hall, 1995.

GOZINTO CHART

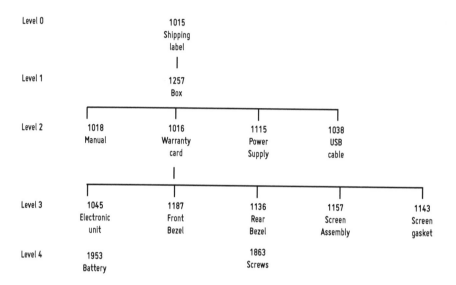

Level 0   1015
       Shipping
       label

Level 1   1257
       Box

Level 2   1018   1016   1115   1038
      Manual   Warranty   Power   USB
              card   Supply   cable

Level 3   1045   1187   1136   1157   1143
     Electronic   Front   Rear   Screen   Screen
       unit   Bezel   Bezel   Assembly   gasket

Level 4   1953   1863
      Battery   Screws

gozinto chart

WHAT IS IT?

The Gozinto chart is a type of tree diagram that shows levels of an assembly. It is a tree representation of a product that shows how the elements required to assemble a product fit together. Gozinto is derived from the phrase "What goes into it?

WHO INVENTED IT?

A. Vazsonyi

WHY USE THIS METHOD?

1. To breakdown a product into its parts.
2. To illustrate the assembly process.
3. To cross-reference parts data with the hierarchical levels of assembly.

CHALLENGES

1. Gozinto chart numbering is by levels and bill of materials or parts list number.

WHEN TO USE THIS METHOD

1. Know Context
2. Know User
3. Frame insights

HOW TO USE THIS METHOD

1. Create a list of all the parts of a product or a system
2. Draw a hierarchy of assembly
3. Provide identification of parts; name and number each part charted.
4. Review and refine

RESOURCES

1. Pen
2. Paper
3. White board
4. Dry erase markers

LINE CHART

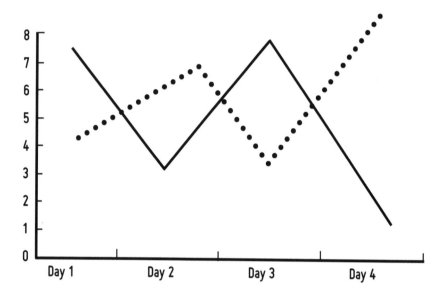

.... Designers working on project in Beijing

———— Designers working on project in London

line chart

WHAT IS IT?
A line chart is a type of chart that is often used to show trends over time

WHY USE THIS METHOD?
1. To display tends over time.

RESOURCES
1. Pen
2. Paper
3. White board
4. Dry erase markers

REFERENCES
1. Neil J. Salkind (2006). Statistics for People who (think They) Hate Statistics: The Excel Edition. page 106.

WHEN TO USE THIS METHOD
1. Frame insights

HOW TO USE THIS METHOD
1. Collect data
2. The horizontal axis is called the X axis and the vertical axis is called the Y axis
3. Draw an X and a Y axis.
4. The Y axis is typically the time intervals such as years or months.
5. Select suitable scales
6. Plot the data points
7. Join the data pints with lines.
8. Add the title and a legend or key if required.

LINKING DIAGRAM

Objectives	Weighting	Responsibility

Objectives (left), Weighting (center), Responsibility (right):

Objectives:
- Reduce SKUs by 25% — 10
- Establish new factory in China — 8
- Decrease returns by 25% — 6
- Increase sales by 25% — 7
- Establish distribution Network in China — 7
- Increase speed to market by 30% — 4
- Reduce manufacturing costs by 25% — 9

Responsibility:
- Industrial Design
- Engineering
- Transportation
- Human Resources
- Manufacturing
- Quality
- Marketing
- Sales
- Sourcing
- Management

linking diagram

WHAT IS IT?

A linking diagram is a graphical method of displaying relationships between factors in data sets.

WHY USE THIS METHOD?

1. To analyze relationships of complex data

RESOURCES

1. Pen
2. Paper
3. White board
4. Dry erase markers

WHEN TO USE THIS METHOD

1. Know Context
2. Know User
3. Frame insights

HOW TO USE THIS METHOD

1. Select a problem to analyze.
2. Team brainstorms two lists of factors that relate to the problem such as outcomes and actions.
3. Team rates the items by importance. 1-10, 10 being most important.
4. Draw lines between related items in each list.
5. Review and refine
6. List insights
7. Take actions based on the insights.

MASLOW'S HIERARCHY OF NEEDS .

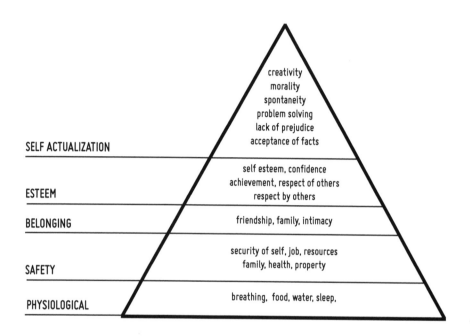

SELF ACTUALIZATION
- creativity
- morality
- spontaneity
- problem solving
- lack of prejudice
- acceptance of facts

ESTEEM
- self esteem, confidence
- achievement, respect of others
- respect by others

BELONGING
- friendship, family, intimacy

SAFETY
- security of self, job, resources
- family, health, property

PHYSIOLOGICAL
- breathing, food, water, sleep,

maslow's hierarchy of needs

WHAT IS IT?

This is a psychological theory proposed by Abraham. The theory has been influential in design and marketing for half a century.

WHO INVENTED IT?

Abraham Maslow 1943

WHY USE THIS METHOD?

1. Maslow believed that these needs play a role in motivating behavior
2. Maslow believed that once these lower-level needs have been met, people move up to the next level of need

CHALLENGES

1. The hierarchy proposed by Maslow is not today universally accepted.
2. Today it is believed that needs are not a linear hierarchy as proposed by Maslow but are more complex, systematic and interconnected.

WHEN TO USE THIS METHOD

1. Frame insights
2. Explore Concepts

HOW TO USE THIS METHOD

The hierarchy as proposed by Maslow is:

1. Self actualization, The highest level,. personal growth and fulfilment
2. Esteem needs. Achievement, status, responsibility, reputation .
3. Social needs. friendships, romantic attachments, and families, social, community, or religious relationships.
4. Security needs. Protection, security, order, law, limits, stability
5. Physiological needs. Air, food, drink, shelter, warmth, sleep.

REFERENCES

1. Maslow, Abraham (1954). Motivation and Personality. New York: Harper. pp. 236. ISBN 0-06-041987-3.
2. Kenrick, D. T., Griskevicius, V., Neuberg, S. L., & Schaller, M. (2010). Renovating the pyramid of needs: Contemporary extensions built upon ancient foundations. Perspectives on Psychological Science, 5, 292. doi: 10.1177/1745691610369469

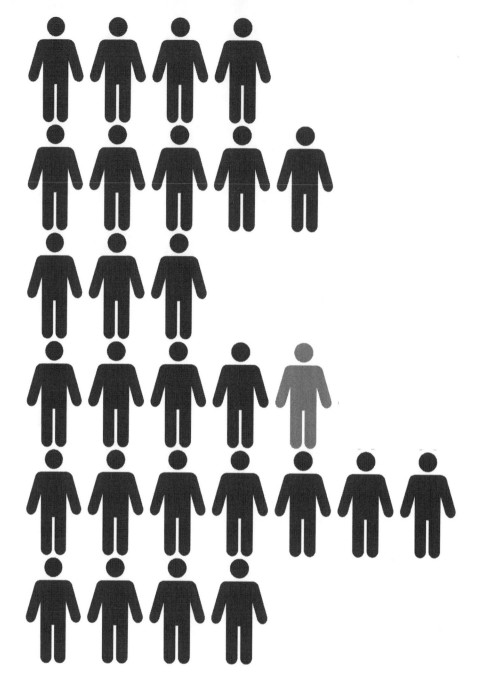

pictogram diagram

WHAT IS IT?

A pictograph is a visual representation of a word or idea. A pictogram conveys it's meaning through it's resemblance to a physical object

WHO INVENTED IT?

Used since ancient times.
George Dow 1936

WHY USE THIS METHOD?

1. Conveys information in an understandable and visual way.
2. Does not require written language to convey meaning.
3. Used where it is necessary to understand the meaning fast such as emergency exits.

WHEN TO USE THIS METHOD

4. Know Context
5. Know User
6. Frame insights

RESOURCES

1. Pen
2. Paper
3. Computer
4. Graphic software

HOW TO USE THIS METHOD

1. Collect data
1. Construct or select suitable pictogram symbol.
1. Plot the data to visually represent the quantity of items.
1. Review and refine

REFERENCES

1. Modley, R. 1976 Handbook of Pictorial Symbols: 3, 250 Examples from International Sources
2. Chambers M. 2004 'Creating icons that really work', in Computer Arts June pp. 38-43
3. Gove, Philip Babcock. (1993). Webster's Third New International Dictionary of the English Language Unabridged. Merriam-Webster Inc. ISBN 0-87779-201-1.

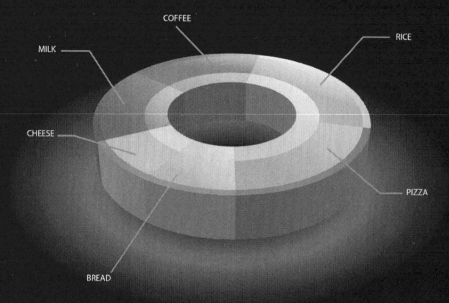

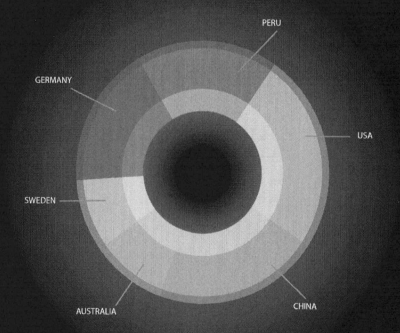

pie chart

WHAT IS IT?
A pie chart is a circle divided into sectors, illustrating proportion.

WHO INVENTED IT?
The earliest known pie chart is believed to be William Playfair's Statistical Breviary of 1801

WHY USE THIS METHOD?
1. The pie chart may be the most widely used statistical chart in business.

CHALLENGES
1. It is difficult to compare data between on or more pie charts.

RESOURCES
1. Pen
2. Paper
3. Compass
4. Protractor
5. Computer
6. Graphics software

WHEN TO USE THIS METHOD
1. Know Context
2. Know User
3. Frame insights

HOW TO USE THIS METHOD
1. Collect data from sources
2. Add the total
3. Calculate the percentage of the total each item.
4. Draw a circle
5. Draw a radius
6. Convert the percentages into angles
7. Each item will equal a percentage of the total and the same percentage of 360 degrees in a circle.
8. Each section is usually colored a different color
9. Label the sections of the pie chart.

REFERENCES
1. Cleveland, William S. (1985). The Elements of Graphing Data. Pacific Grove, CA: Wadsworth & Advanced Book Program. ISBN 0-534-03730-5.
2. Harris, Robert L. (1999). Information Graphics: A comprehensive Illustrated Reference. Oxford University Press. ISBN 0-19-513532-6.

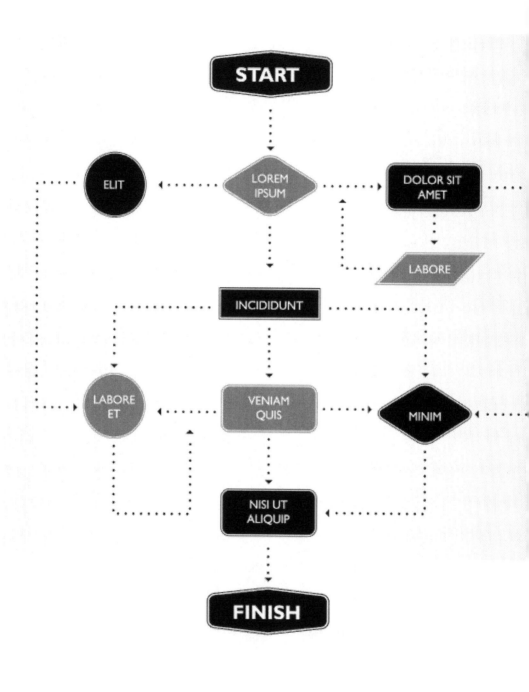

process flow diagram

WHAT IS IT?
A process flowchart is a type of diagram that represents a process, showing the steps as boxes

WHO INVENTED IT?
Frank Gilbreth, American Society of Mechanical Engineers,1921

WHY USE THIS METHOD?
1. To represent a flow of process or decisions or both.

CHALLENGES
1. Use standard symbols.
2. Arrows should show the direction of flow.
3. A junction is indicated by two incoming and one outgoing line.
4. The two most common types of boxes are for a process step and for a decisions.

RESOURCES
1. Pen
2. Paper
3. White board
4. Dry erase markers.

WHEN TO USE THIS METHOD
1. Know Context
2. Frame insights

HOW TO USE THIS METHOD
1. Define the process boundaries
2. Complete the big picture first.
3. Draw a start box.
4. Draw the first box below the start box. Ask, 'What happens first?'.
5. Add further boxes below the previous box, Ask 'What happens next?'.
6. Connect the boxes with arrows
7. Describe the process to be charted
8. Review.

REFERENCES
1. Frank Bunker Gilbreth, Lillian Moller Gilbreth (1921) Process Charts. American Society of Mechanical Engineers.
2. Bohl, Rynn: "Tools for Structured and Object-Oriented Design", Prentice Hall, 2007.

PRODUCT LIFECYCLE MAP

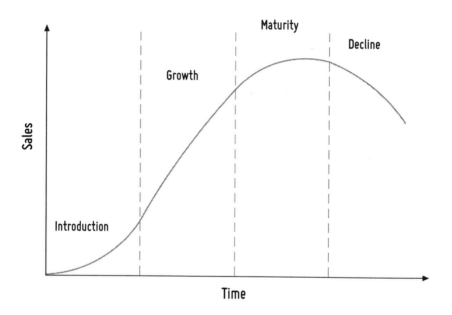

product life cycle map

WHAT IS IT?
A product lifecycle map shows the sales of a product over time. there are four stages in the life of a product, the introduction stage, the growth stage, the maturity stage and the decline stage.

WHO INVENTED IT?
Geoffrey Moore 1991

WHY USE THIS METHOD?
1. For strategic planning

CHALLENGES
1. The performance of each product will not be the same so review the performance of a product category.

WHEN TO USE THIS METHOD
1. Define intent
2. Frame insights

HOW TO USE THIS METHOD
1. Collect data
2. Map data
3. Project data

RESOURCES
1. Pen
2. Paper
3. White board
4. Dry erase markers.

REFERENCES
1. Karnie, Arie; Reich, Yoram (2011). Managing the Dynamic of New Product Development Processes. A new Product Lifecycle Management Paradigm. Springer. p. 13. ISBN 978-0-85729-569-9.
2. Saaksvuori, Antti (2008). Product Lifecycle Management. Springer. ISBN 978-3-540-78173-8.
3. Stark, John (2006). Global Product: Strategy, Product Lifecycle Management and the Billion Customer Question. Springer. ISBN 978-1-84628-915-6.

visual dissonance

WHAT IS IT?
This method identifies inconsistences in an existing design that may serve as a focus for improving the design.

WHO INVENTED IT?
John Chris Jones 1992

WHY USE THIS METHOD?
1. A method that can be used individually or by a team to identify ways of improving an existing design.

WHEN TO USE THIS METHOD
1. Define intent
2. Frame insights

HOW TO USE THIS METHOD
1. Present some physical samples or photographs of a product or video of a service or experience to your design team.
2. Brainstorm with your team conflicts between the existing design and it's intended purpose or usability.
3. Brainstorm ways of improving the design to remove the conflicts.

RESOURCES
1. Product samples
2. Camera
3. White board
4. Post-it notes

REFERENCES
1. Jones, John Christopher, Design Methods: seeds of human futures, John Wiley & Sons Ltd., London, 1970; 2nd edition, John Wiley & Sons Ltd., 1992

Chapter 6
Explore ideas
how is this idea to start?

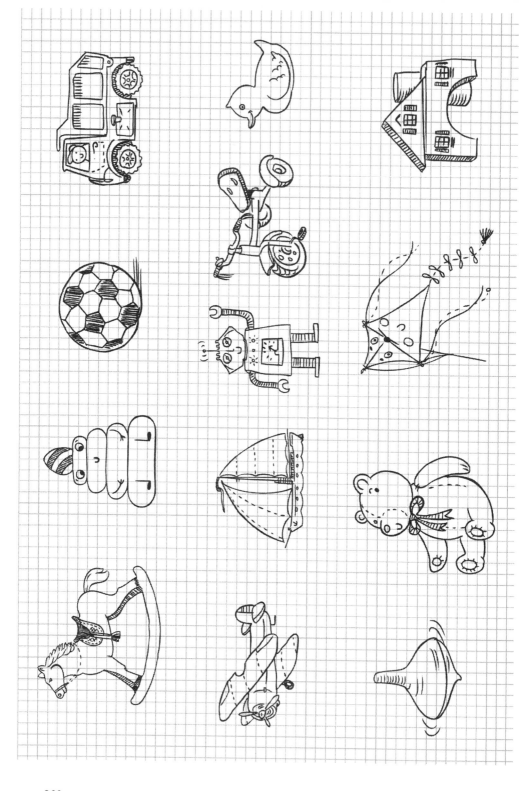

10 x 10 sketch method

WHAT IS IT?

This method is an approach to making early concept generation sketching more efficient in use of time than the method that stresses finished sketches early in the design process. It allows more time to explore ideas and so stresses the quality of thinking and the final solution. The 10 x 10 method involves creating ten rows with ten thumbnail sketches per row on each page.

WHY USE THIS METHOD?

1. It allows more exploration of alternative ideas in a shorter time
2. May lead to a final concept which is a better design than traditional approaches.
3. Prevents sketches from becoming jewelry in the mind of the designer and more important than the quality of the final design solution.

CHALLENGES

1. This method takes discipline

WHEN TO USE THIS METHOD

1. Explore Concepts

HOW TO USE THIS METHOD

1. Traditional design concept exploration involves a designer producing six to 12 alternative design concepts presented as attractive renderings
2. This method involves a designer making ten rows of ten simple fast cartoon like sketches per page.
3. Each sketch should be no larger than one inch by one inch.
4. The designer produces 5 to 20 pages of very fast sketches during first phase of concept exploration
5. Designs are reviewed and ranked by the design team following a discussion and presentation by the designer and a relatively small number are selected for iteration, recombination and further development.
6. At the next stage more finished and larger concept sketches are produced

RESOURCES

1. Paper
2. Fine line pens
3. Sharpie markers

alexander's method

WHAT IS IT?

The Alexander Method is a way of simplifying complex relationships and interactions in a large project and presenting them visually so as to be able to better understand their relationships and hierarchy of importance.

WHO INVENTED IT?

Christopher Wolfgang Alexander 1963

WHY USE THIS METHOD?

1. It is a way of understanding complex relationships and prioritizing them in a large project.

CHALLENGES

1. This is a mechanistic approach to design problems.
2. Value judgements are inevitable

WHEN TO USE THIS METHOD

1. Define intent
2. Know Context
3. Know User
4. Frame insights
5. Explore Concepts
6. Make Plans
7. Deliver Offering

HOW TO USE THIS METHOD

1. Interview users and capture hundreds of ideas and experiences in words.
2. Number each interview statement.
3. Produce a number of dependent statements under the headings If, when, where, while, because.
4. An expert team reviews the statements and identifies those that are strongly connected.
5. An interaction matrix is created with the statement numbers on vertical and horizontal axes.
6. Analyze each pair of factors to determine which are dependent and which independent.
7. Label each relationship as positive, negative or neutral depending on whether they support, inhibit or have no effect on each other.
8. A network diagram is produced showing the relationships of factors which are most heavily dependent.
9. Reduce the complex task to a number of important issues related as clusters.

REFERENCES

1. Community and Privacy, with Serge Chermayeff (1963)
2. Grabow, Stephen: Christopher Alexander: The Search for a New Paradigm in Architecture, Routledge & Kegan Paul, London and Boston, 1983.
3. Alexander, C. (1964). Notes On The Synthesis Of Form. Mass., Harvard University Press.

attribute analysis

WHAT IS IT?
This is a method that helps to generate concepts by combining or associating attributes.

WHO INVENTED IT?
Fritz Zwicky Caltech 1966
Norris, K.W. 1963

WHY USE THIS METHOD?
1. To help expand the possible solutions to a design problem.

RESOURCES
1. Pen
2. Paper
3. White board
4. Dry erase markers
5. Post-it-notes

WHEN TO USE THIS METHOD
6. Explore Concepts

HOW TO USE THIS METHOD
1. Define your design problem
2. Define the attributes of the design solution.
3. Create a matrix
4. List each attribute as a column heading on the top horizontal axis of the matrix
5. An attribute may be a part, property, quality or element of a design such as dimensions, color, weight, style, speed of service, skills available
6. Write down as many variations of each attributes as possible in the column below the attribute
7. Select one attribute from each column and combine them into a concept.
8. This can be done by intuition or randomly.
9. Develop the best ideas.

REFERENCES
1. Bailey, K.(1994) Typologies and Taxonomies – An Introduction to Classification Techniques, Sage University Papers: Thousand Oaks.

brainstorming:
analogies and metaphors

WHAT IS IT?
A method to help clarify an issue when exploring complex ideas. An analogy is a way of showing similarities between two different things. a metaphor is a representation of something.

WHO INVENTED IT?
Ava S, Butler 1996

WHY USE THIS METHOD?
1. Unstructured meetings waste time by trying to discuss all aspects of an issue at once.
2. This method saves time and improves the outcomes and efficiency of meetings.
3. Useful when discussing complex issues

RESOURCES
1. Paper
2. Pens
3. Whiteboard
4. Dry erase markers

WHEN TO USE THIS METHOD
1. Know Context
2. Know User
3. Frame insights
4. Explore Concepts

HOW TO USE THIS METHOD
1. Define the problem to be addressed.
2. The moderator introduces the problem and the method.
3. The moderator gives the group five minutes to consider appropriate analogies and metaphors.
4. Each participant presents their best analogies and metaphors to the group.
5. The group selects the best analogies and metaphors.
6. Summarize learnings.

REFERENCES
1. Butler, Ava S. (1996) Teamthink Publisher: Mcgraw Hill ISBN 0070094330
2. Clark , Charles Hutchinson. Brainstorming: The Dynamic New Way to Create Successful Ideas Publisher: Classic Business Bookshelf (November 23, 2010) ISBN-10: 1608425614 ISBN-13: 978-1608425617
3. Rawlinson J. Geoffrey Creative Thinking and Brainstorming. Jaico Publishing House (April 30, 2005) ISBN-10: 8172243480 ISBN-13: 978-8172243487

benjamin franklin method

WHAT IS IT?
A method developed by Benjamin Franklin for making decisions.

WHO INVENTED IT?
Benjamin Franklin 1772

WHY USE THIS METHOD?
1. It is simple
2. It was developed and used by Benjamin Franklin who was a successful decision maker.

WHEN TO USE THIS METHOD
1. Explore Concepts

RESOURCES
1. Pen
2. Paper
3. White board
4. Dry erase markers
5. Post-it-notes

HOW TO USE THIS METHOD
Quote from a letter from Benjamin Franklin to Joseph Priestley London, September 19, 1772

"To get over this, my Way is, to divide half a Sheet of Paper by a Line into two Columns, writing over the one Pro, and over the other Con. Then during three or four Days Consideration I put down under the different Heads short Hints of the different Motives that at different Times occur to me for or against the Measure. When I have thus got them all together in one View, I endeavour to estimate their respective Weights; and where I find two, one on each side, that seem equal, I strike them both out: If I find a Reason pro equal to some two Reasons con, I strike out the three. If I judge some two Reasons con equal to some three Reasons pro, I strike out the five; and thus proceeding I find at length where the Ballance lies; and if after a Day or two of farther Consideration nothing new that is of Importance occurs on either side, I come to a Determination accordingly.

And tho' the Weight of Reasons cannot be taken with the Precision of Algebraic Quantities, yet when each is thus considered separately and comparatively, and the whole lies before me, I think I can judge better, and am less likely to take a rash Step; and in fact I have found great Advantage from this kind of Equation, in what may be called Moral or Prudential Algebra"

brainstorming: crawford slip method

WHAT IS IT?

The Crawford Slip method is a form of brainstorming that was developed in the 1920s and may have been the inspiration for most forms of brainstorming today. It was the origin of the method of brainstorming most common today. A moderator defines a problem statement, then participants record their ideas on 3 × 5 index cards.

WHO INVENTED IT?

The Crawford slip method was developed in the late 1920's by Dr. C. Crawford of the University of Southern California

WHY USE THIS METHOD?

1. Any size group
2. Commonly used for 50 to 200 participants but can be used for up to 5,000 people.
3. Any seating arrangement.
4. Broader participation (includes less expressive participants).
5. Large quantity of ideas.
6. Good for sensitive topics since participants' input is anonymous, without team interaction.
7. Easier process of sorting ideas.

CHALLENGES

1. May be a slow process.
2. Written ideas may need to be explained verbally.
3. Written ideas may be stated as a word if a detailed description would be too long.
4. All members participate.

WHEN TO USE THIS METHOD

1. Explore Concepts

HOW TO USE THIS METHOD

1. Define the problem
2. Distribute 3 inch by 5 inch blank index cards to each team member. 20 cards each may be a suitable number.
3. The moderator writes the problem statement on a white board.
4. Participants spend 20 minutes to 40 minutes generating ideas and describing one idea per index card with sketches or written descriptions. One sentence or idea per card.
5. The cards are returned to the moderator and spread out on a large table.
6. The cards are sorted into between 3 and 10 large categories. The categories depend on the problem and are generated by the team through discussion.
7. The categories are prioritized.

RESOURCES

1. Pens
2. Paper
3. 3 X 5 inch index cards

REFERENCES

1. Dettmer H, W. Brainpower Networking Using the Crawford Slip Method. Publisher: Trafford (October 2003) ISBN-10: 141200909X ISBN-13: 978-1412009096

brainstorming: disney method

WHAT IS IT?

The Disney method is a parallel thinking technique. It allows a team to discuss an issue from four perspectives. It involves parallel thinking to analyze a problem, generate ideas, evaluate ideas, and to create a strategy. It is a method used in workshops. The four thinking perspectives are – Spectators, Dreamers, Realist's and Critics.

WHO INVENTED IT?

Dilts, 1991

WHY USE THIS METHOD?

1. Allows the group top discuss a problem from four different perspectives

CHALLENGES

1. An alternative to De Bono Six hat Method.
2. Will deliver a workable solution quickly.

WHEN TO USE THIS METHOD

1. Explore Concepts

HOW TO USE THIS METHOD

1. At the end of each of the four sessions the participants leave the room and then at a later time reenter the room then assuming the personas and perspectives of the next group. Time taken is often 60 to 90 minutes in total.
2. The spectator's view. Puts the problem in an external context. How would a consultant, a customer or an outside observer view the problem?

3. The Dreamers view. Looking for an ideal solution. What would our dream solution for this be? What if? Unconstrained brainstorm. Defer judgement. Divergent thinking. What do we desire? If we could have unlimited resources what would we do? They list their ideas on the white board.
4. Realists view. The realists are convergent thinkers. How can we turn the dreamer's views into reality? Looking for ideas that are feasible, profitable, customer focused and can be implemented within 18 months. They look through the dreamer's ideas on the white board and narrow them down to a short list, discuss them and choose the single best idea and create an implementation plan. What steps are necessary to implement this idea? Who can approve it, how much funding is needed? They draw the plan on the whiteboard and then leave the room.
5. The Critics view. What are the risks and obstacles? Who would oppose this plan? What could go wrong? Refine, improve or reject. Be constructive. This group defines the risks and obstacles, make some suggestions and write down these ideas on the white board.

RESOURCES

1. White board
2. Dry erase markers.
3. Pens
4. Post-it-notes.
5. A private room

We Wish You a MERRY CHRISTMAS and Happy New Year

When dreams come true
BELIEVE IT

brainstorming: greeting cards

WHAT IS IT?
This is a group creativity method that uses greeting cards as a focus to stimulate ideas.

WHO INVENTED IT?
James Pickens 1981

WHY USE THIS METHOD?
1. It is a way to build team collaboration and stimulate ideas.

RESOURCES
2. Paste
3. Scissors
4. Magazines
5. Thick A3 or A4 paper
6. Felt-tipped pens

REFERENCES
1. Clark , Charles Hutchinson. Brainstorming: The Dynamic New Way to Create Successful Ideas Publisher: Classic Business Bookshelf (November 23, 2010) ISBN-10: 1608425614 ISBN-13: 978-1608425617
2. Rawlinson J. Geoffrey Creative Thinking and Brainstorming. Jaico Publishing House (April 30, 2005) ISBN-10: 8172243480 ISBN-13: 978-8172243487

WHEN TO USE THIS METHOD
1. Explore Concepts

HOW TO USE THIS METHOD
1. The moderator introduces the method
2. Break the large group into smaller groups of 3 to 5 people.
3. Supply each group with the materials listed under "resources"
4. Each participant cuts out 10 pictures that they like
5. Each group creates 2 or 3 greeting cards with their own message using the images and materials.
6. Each group presents their cards to the larger group.
7. The moderator introduces a problem statement and the groups use their cards to stimulate ideas for solutions.
8. Pass cards to next group and repeat.
9. When this process is complete review all the solutions with the larger group and select preferred directions.

brainstorming:
nominal group method

WHAT IS IT?
The nominal group method is a brainstorming method that is designed to encourage participation of all members of the team and minimizes the possibility of more vocal members from dominating the discussion.

WHO INVENTED IT?
William Fox

WHY USE THIS METHOD?
1. To define and prioritize problems or opportunities
2. To understand the best solution to a problem
3. To create a plan to implement an opportunity

RESOURCES
1. White board
2. Dry erase markers
3. Blank postcards

WHEN TO USE THIS METHOD
4. Frame insights
5. Explore Concepts

REFERENCES
1. The Memory Jogger II: A Pocket Guide of Tools for Continuous Improvement and Effective Planning Michael Brassard (Author), Diane Ritter (Author), Francine Oddo (Editor) 1st edition (January 15, 1994) ISBN-10: 1879364441 ISBN-13: 978-1879364448

HOW TO USE THIS METHOD
1. Distribute information about the process to participants before the meeting.
2. Participants drop anonymous suggestions into an unmonitored suggestion box written on blank postcards.
3. The suggestions are distributed to participants before the meeting so that they can think about them.
4. In the meeting the moderator writes the suggestions on to a white board
5. Each participant has the opportunity to speak in support or against any of the suggestions.
6. The moderator leads the team in to clarify each idea,
7. The moderator instructs each person to work silently and independently for five minutes, recording as many ideas, thoughts, or answers as possible on paper.
8. The moderator asks the group to list 5 to 10 ideas that the like the most, in order of importance, and to pass them to the moderator.
9. The moderator counts up the number of votes for each idea.
10. Each participant is given a number of votes that they record on blank postcards which are collected face down and tallied.

brainstorming: out of the box

WHAT IS IT?

This is a method to perform out-of-the box brainstorming to generate outrageous and wild ideas.

WHY USE THIS METHOD?

1. To generate wild ideas
2. To promote creative thinking among participants.

RESOURCES

1. Pen
2. Paper
3. White board
4. Dry erase markers
5. Post-it-notes

CHALLENGES

1. Avoid persona representations that may be harmful.
2. Groupthink
3. Not enough good ideas
4. Taking turns
5. Freeloading
6. Inhibition
7. Lack of critical thinking
8. A group that is too large competes for attention.

WHEN TO USE THIS METHOD

1. Explore Concepts

HOW TO USE THIS METHOD

1. The moderator introduces this method.
2. The moderator shows the team several wild or out of the box ideas.
3. Participants generate concepts stressing that they must be wild and out of the box.
4. The moderator records the ideas on a white board.
5. The team reviews the ideas and selects some for further development and bringing back to reality.

RESOURCES

1. Pen
2. Paper
3. White board
4. Dry erase markers
5. Post-it-notes

REFERENCES

1. Clark , Charles Hutchinson. Brainstorming: The Dynamic New Way to Create Successful Ideas Publisher: Classic Business Bookshelf (November 23, 2010) ISBN-10: 1608425614 ISBN-13: 978-1608425617
2. Rawlinson J. Geoffrey Creative Thinking and Brainstorming. Jaico Publishing House (April 30, 2005) ISBN-10: 8172243480 ISBN-13: 978-8172243487

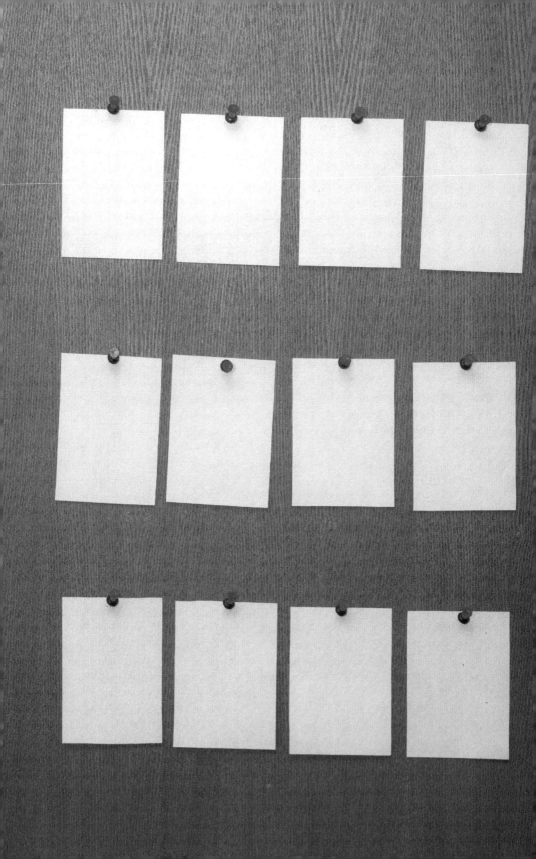

brainstorming: pin cards

WHAT IS IT?

The pin cards technique is a brainwriting process to generate ideas on colored cards that are sorted into groups and discussed. This method allows participants to think of more ideas during the writing process. This method can generate more ideas than some other brainstorming methods.

WHO INVENTED IT?

Wolfgang Schnelle

WHY USE THIS METHOD?

1.   To generate ideas to solve a problem
2.   To produce many ideas quickly and without filtering from other participants.

CHALLENGES

1.   Cards need to be passed on quickly
2.   Participants may feel time stressed.
3.   Some participants may want to make their ideas confidential.

RESOURCES

1.   Colored blank index cards
2.   Pins
3.   Pin Board
4.   Pens
5.   Markers

WHEN TO USE THIS METHOD

1.   Explore Concepts

HOW TO USE THIS METHOD

1.   The moderator writes the problem statement on a white board.
2.   The participants should be seated around a large table.
3.   The moderator distributes 10 cards of the same color to each participant.
4.   Each participant receives different-colored cards.
5.   Participants record one idea per card.
6.   Ideas can be a cartoon sketch or a sentence
7.   Completed cards are passed to the person on the participant's right hand side.
8.   Participants can review cards from a person on their left hand side.
9.   After 30 to 45 minutes all the participants pin the cards that they have to a wall.
10. Each participant should aim to produce at least 40 ideas.
11. The team sorts the cards into a number of groups by association. The type of association are determined by the group.
12. The participants prioritize the groups and combine the ideas in the favored group for further development.

REFERENCES

1.   Nancy R. Tague .The Quality Toolbox, Second Edition. SQ Quality Press; 2 edition (March 30, 2005) ISBN-10: 0873896394 ISBN-13: 978-0873896399

brainstorming: pool method

WHAT IS IT?

Brainstorming is one of the oldest,fastest and most widely used creativity methods. Brainstorming does need to be undertaken by experts. It can be undertaken as a group or individually. Osborn believed that brainstorming as a group was most effective. Recent research has questioned this assumption. It should be used to address a single problem. Brainstorming is worthwhile when it is part of a larger process of design.

WHO INVENTED IT?

Alex Faickney Osborn 1953

WHY USE THIS METHOD?

1. It is useful for generating new types of solutions to problems.
2. It can be used to overcome creative blocks.
3. There is group buy-in to a design direction.

CHALLENGES

1. Groupthink
2. Not enough good ideas
3. Taking turns
4. Freeloading
5. Inhibition
6. Lack of critical thinking
7. A group that is too large competes for attention.

WHEN TO USE THIS METHOD

1. Explore Concepts

HOW TO USE THIS METHOD

1. Define the problem
2. Moderator briefs the design team.
3. A group size of 4 to 20 people is optimum.
4. Supply each team member with a pile of 50 blank index cards
5. Give the team 30 minutes to create 10 ideas each.
6. Each team member describes their ideas and places the cards with the ideas, one per card in a central pool .
7. Give the team another 30 minutes. Each team members can select one or more ideas to develop which have been created by another team member from the central pool to develop in the second session.

brainstorming: post-it

WHAT IS IT?
It is a method that uses combinations of brainstormed words to generate ideas.

WHY USE THIS METHOD?
1. New ideas start with making new connections.

RESOURCES
1. Whiteboard
2. Dry erase markers
3. Post-it notes
4. Pens
5. Paper
6. Markers

WHEN TO USE THIS METHOD
1. Explore Concepts

HOW TO USE THIS METHOD
1. Ask your team to write all the words that they associate with the problem.
2. One word per post-it-note.
3. Spread the post-it-notes over a wall.
4. As the second level of brainstorming generate ideas based on combinations of words
5. Brainstorm a list of "how to" solutions based on the ideas.

brainstorming: rolestorming

WHAT IS IT?
Rolestorming is a brainstorming method where participants adopt other people's identity while brainstorming.

WHO INVENTED IT?
Rick Griggs1980s

WHY USE THIS METHOD?
1. Helps reduce inhibitions which some team members may have in suggesting innovative solutions.

CHALLENGES
1. Avoid persona representations that may be harmful.
2. Groupthink
3. Not enough good ideas
4. Taking turns
5. Freeloading
6. Inhibition
7. Lack of critical thinking
8. A group that is too large competes for attention.

WHEN TO USE THIS METHOD
1. Explore Concepts

HOW TO USE THIS METHOD
1. Select moderator
2. Conduct a traditional brainstorming session
3. At the conclusion of the first brainstorming session the moderator identifies a number of identities to be used for the second session
4. The identities can be any person not in the brainstorming group such as a competitor, a famous person, a boss. They should be known to the team members.
5. The Moderator asks some questions
   How would this identity solve the problem?
   What would this persona see as the problem?
   Where would this persona see the problem?
   Why would the persona see a problem?
6. Brainstorm in character.
7. Use words such as "My persona"
8. Share ideas.

REFERENCES
1. Clark , Charles Hutchinson. Brainstorming: The Dynamic New Way to Create Successful Ideas Publisher: Classic Business Bookshelf (November 23, 2010) ISBN-10: 1608425614 ISBN-13: 978-1608425617
2. Rawlinson J. Geoffrey Creative Thinking and Brainstorming. Jaico Publishing House (April 30, 2005) ISBN-10: 8172243480 ISBN-13: 978-8172243487

brainstorming: starbusting

WHAT IS IT?
Starbursting generates questions to clarify issues, probe for potential solutions, or verify resource requirements.

WHO INVENTED IT?
Alex Faickney Osborn 1953

WHY USE THIS METHOD?
1. To identify potential problem areas
2. Useful for generating new types of solutions to problems.

CHALLENGES
1. No evaluation of questions is allowed during the starbursting process.
2. Groupthink
3. Not enough good ideas
4. Taking turns
5. Freeloading
6. Inhibition
7. Lack of critical thinking
8. A group that is too large competes
9. for attention.

RESOURCES
1. Pens
2. Post-it-notes
3. A flip chart
4. White board or wall
5. Refreshments.

WHEN TO USE THIS METHOD
1. Explore Concepts

HOW TO USE THIS METHOD
1. The fist step is to define a problem to be explored or to review a set of previously brainstormed ideas.
2. The participants may ask as many questions as they would like without other participants judging them.
3. Participants write their questions on 3 × 5 inch index cards.
4. The moderator collects the questions and writes them on a white board.
5. The team organizes the questions into related groups and prioritizes them

RESOURCES
1. Pens
2. 3 x5 inch blank index cards
3. White board or wall
4. Refreshments.

REFERENCES
1. Clark , Charles Hutchinson. Brainstorming: The Dynamic New Way to Create Successful Ideas Publisher: Classic Business Bookshelf (November 23, 2010) ISBN-10: 1608425614 ISBN-13: 978-1608425617
2. Rawlinson J. Geoffrey Creative Thinking and Brainstorming. Jaico Publishing House (April 30, 2005) ISBN-10: 8172243480 ISBN-13: 978-8172243487

STP CHART

SITUATION	TARGET	PROPOSAL

brainstorming: stp method

WHAT IS IT?
STP is a brainstorming method designed to help define ways of reaching a goal.

WHO INVENTED IT?
Ava S Butler 1996

WHY USE THIS METHOD?
1. To generate new ideas

CHALLENGES
1. Groupthink
2. Not enough good ideas
3. Taking turns
4. Freeloading
5. Inhibition
6. Lack of critical thinking
7. A group that is too large competes for attention.

RESOURCES
1. Pens
2. Post-it-notes
3. A flip chart
4. White board or wall
5. Refreshments.

REFERENCES
1. Butler, Ava S. (1996) Teamthink Publisher: Mcgraw Hill ISBN 0070094330
2. Clark, Charles Hutchinson. Brainstorming: The Dynamic New Way to Create Successful Ideas Publisher: Classic Business Bookshelf (November 23, 2010) ISBN-10: 1608425614 ISBN-13: 978-1608425617
3. Rawlinson J. Geoffrey Creative Thinking and Brainstorming. Jaico Publishing House (April 30, 2005) ISBN-10: 8172243480

WHEN TO USE THIS METHOD
1. Explore Concepts

HOW TO USE THIS METHOD
1. The moderator writes three headings on a white board. Situation, target and proposal.
2. The moderator reviews the rules of brainstorming. Go for quantity.
3. The moderator asks the question "What do you see as the current situation?"
4. When all ideas have been recorded the moderator asks "Which comments need clarification?"
5. After team members provide clarification the moderator asks " What is our ideal goal?"
6. After all ideas have been recorded and clarifies the moderator asks" What is our preferred target?"
7. After the team votes and a preferred target is selected the moderator asks "How can we get from our current situation to our preferred target?"
8. After all ideas have been recorded and clarified the team selects a preferred way to get to the target by voting.

brainstorming: up and down

WHAT IS IT?

This is a brainstorming method that creates ideas from the top and lowest employees of an organization

WHO INVENTED IT?

Alex Faickney Osborn 1953

WHY USE THIS METHOD?

1. It is useful for generating new types of solutions to problems.
2. Brainstorming allows each person in a group to better understand a problem.
3. It can be used to overcome creative blocks.
4. There is group buy-in to a design direction.

CHALLENGES

1. Groupthink
2. Not enough good ideas
3. Taking turns
4. Freeloading
5. Inhibition
6. Lack of critical thinking
7. A group that is too large competes for attention.

WHEN TO USE THIS METHOD

1. Explore Concepts

HOW TO USE THIS METHOD

1. Ask your team to brainstorm the viewpoint of the CEO
2. Ask your team to brainstorm the problem from the viewpoint of the lowest employee
3. How would the problem be different from their perspectives?
4. Formulate how to statements.

RESOURCES

1. Pens
2. Post-it-notes
3. A flip chart
4. White board or wall
5. Refreshments.

REFERENCES

1. Clark , Charles Hutchinson. Brainstorming: The Dynamic New Way to Create Successful Ideas Publisher: Classic Business Bookshelf (November 23, 2010) ISBN-10: 1608425614 ISBN-13: 978-1608425617
2. Rawlinson J. Geoffrey Creative Thinking and Brainstorming. Jaico Publishing House (April 30, 2005) ISBN-10: 8172243480 ISBN-13: 978-8172243487

brainstorming: wishful thinking

WHAT IS IT?

This method gives your team members an opportunity to propose possible outcomes that they would like to see and the team to brainstorm each team member's wish.

WHY USE THIS METHOD?

1. It is useful for generating new types of solutions to problems.
2. Brainstorming allows each person in a group to better understand a problem.
3. It can be used to overcome creative blocks.
4. There is group buy-in to a design direction.

CHALLENGES

1. Some team members may find the initial wishes challenging.

WHEN TO USE THIS METHOD

2. Frame insights
3. Explore Concepts

RESOURCES

1. Pens
2. Post-it-notes
3. A flip chart
4. White board or wall
5. Refreshments.

HOW TO USE THIS METHOD

1. Define the problem.
2. Moderator provides an overview of the method.
3. The participants each generate one wish. An example may be : 'We should have more flexible work hours"
4. The moderator records the statements on a white board
5. In a second stage of the brainstorm which can be called "reality check" The participants review the wish list and suggest how each wish may be actualized in a practical way. Ask: "How can we really do this?" "What resource could be used?" "What could happen if we try this?"
6. The team reviews the second list and votes on their preferred directions for further development.

REFERENCES

1. Clark , Charles Hutchinson. Brainstorming: The Dynamic New Way to Create Successful Ideas Publisher: Classic Business Bookshelf (November 23, 2010) ISBN-10: 1608425614 ISBN-13: 978-1608425617
2. Rawlinson J. Geoffrey Creative Thinking and Brainstorming. Jaico Publishing House (April 30, 2005) ISBN-10: 8172243480 ISBN-13: 978-8172243487

BUSINESS MATRIX ANALYSIS

PRODUCTS	CUSTOMER NEEDS	MARKET SECTOR	PROMOTION METHODS	MANUFACT. METHODS	DISTRIBUT. METHODS

business matrix analysis

WHAT IS IT?
This is a method that helps to generate concepts by combining or connecting business related factors

WHO INVENTED IT?
Fritz Zwicky Caltech 1966
Norris, K.W. 1963

WHY USE THIS METHOD?
1. To help expand the possible solutions to a design problem.

RESOURCES
1. Pen
2. Paper
3. White board
4. Dry erase markers
5. Post-it-notes

WHEN TO USE THIS METHOD
1. Explore Concepts

HOW TO USE THIS METHOD
1. Define your design problem
2. Define the business, user and market factors of the design solution such as market sectors, customer needs, products, promotional methods
3. Create a matrix
4. List each factor as a column heading on the top horizontal axis of the matrix
5. Write down as many variations of each factor as possible in the column below the attribute
6. Select one factor from each column and combine them into a concept.
7. This can be done by intuition or randomly.
8. Develop the best ideas.

REFERENCES
1. Bailey, K.(1994) Typologies and Taxonomies – An Introduction to Classification Techniques, Sage University Papers: Thousand Oaks.

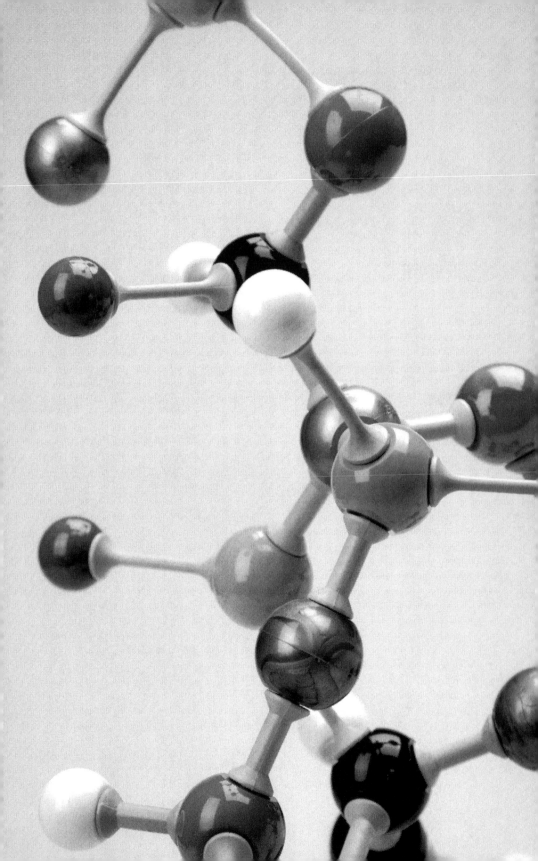

cluster analysis

WHAT IS IT?
Cluster analysis is a method for organizing similar items or ideas and combining them for further development.

WHY USE THIS METHOD?
1. To classify ideas into natural groups on the basis of similarities.
2. To identify the most important factors to focus on for development.
1.

RESOURCES
1. Pen
2. Paper
3. White board
4. Dry erase markers
5. Post-it-notes
6.

SEE ALSO
1. Affinity diagrams

WHEN TO USE THIS METHOD
1. Explore Concepts

HOW TO USE THIS METHOD
1. The team brainstorms ideas.
2. 100 to 150 ideas is a good number for this method.
3. The team look at all items and suggests general or topical headings for similar items. They become the cluster names .
4. The moderator records all suggested cluster names and asks participants to sort or organize items to be placed under each cluster name.
5. After all items have been sorted the team votes of the priorities of the groups to focus on for further development.

303

collective notebook

WHAT IS IT?

The collective note book method is a method of generating ideas for products, services and experiences using a team of people working independently. The idea generation takes place over a four week period.

WHO INVENTED IT?

John Haefele, Proctor and Gamble 1962
Pearson 1979

WHY USE THIS METHOD?

1. The extended period allows deeper exploration of ideas through incubation.
2.

CHALLENGES

1. Requires time
2. Can involve a lot of work to coordinate

WHEN TO USE THIS METHOD

1. Explore Concepts

RESOURCES

2. Pens
3. Note pad
4. Cameras

HOW TO USE THIS METHOD

1. Each participant records one idea on one page in a notebook for one month.
2. Experts give each participant more information at regular intervals over the one month period.
3. At the end of the one month period each participant selects their best idea and summarizes their thoughts.
4. The notebooks are collected.
5. The notebooks are reviewed and a summary of their contents is made.
6. Participants are shown the summary document.
7. A group discussion is organized and conducted with all of the participants and the design team and stakeholders.

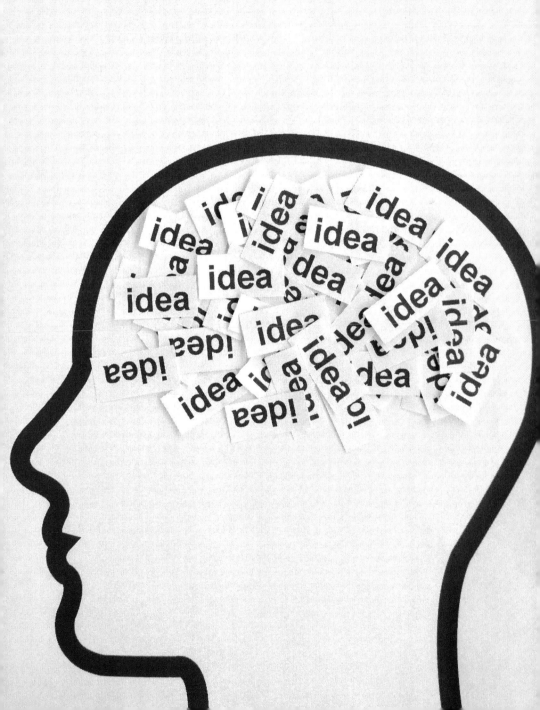

competencies model

WHAT IS IT?
It is a method for generating solutions to problems based on the Osborn–Parnes CPS process.

WHO INVENTED IT?
Reali, 2009

WHY USE THIS METHOD?
1. A flexible method
2. Uses both divergent and convergent thinking at each phase.

WHEN TO USE THIS METHOD
1. Define intent
2. Know Context
3. Know User
4. Frame insights
5. Explore Concepts

RESOURCES
1. Pens
2. Paper
3. Post it notes
4. White board
5. Dry erase markers
6. Video camera

HOW TO USE THIS METHOD
1. Facilitate
2. Imagine the Future
3. Find the Questions
4. Generate Ideas
5. Craft Solutions
6. Explore Acceptance
7. Plan for Action

306

consensus decision making

WHAT IS IT?

The consensus decision making method is a process in which all team participants openly communicate their ideas and exchange their points of view. The gaol is for all team participants to accept and support a team decision even though some may not completely agree with it.

WHO INVENTED IT?

Quakers,used the technique from the 17th century. There is some evidence of consensus decision making in the bible.

WHY USE THIS METHOD?

1. To reach agreement on a proposed action or next step in a problem-solving effort.
2. To gain general agreement and support on a particular idea or issue.
3. To allow team participants the opportunity to express and defend their point of view.
4. To avoid conflict or rush to a decision.

CHALLENGES

1. Consensus is reached after all participants have presented their views.
2. Participants fully understand, accept, and will support the team decision.
3. Reaching consensus often requires greater individual participation, clear communication, and some compromise on well- considered decision

WHEN TO USE THIS METHOD

1. Explore Concepts
2. Make Plans

HOW TO USE THIS METHOD

1. The team brainstorms a list of ideas.
2. Team members clarify all issues, share views, and listen to other ideas or concerns.
3. It is important that all team members actively participate in the discussion.
4. After all information has been shared and alternatives considered, the team develops general agreement and reaches compromise.
5. The team creates a statement that all participants understand and are willing to support.

REFERENCES

1. The World's Business Cultures and How to Unlock Them 2008 Barry Tomalin, Mike Nicks pg. 109 "Consensus or individually-driven decision making" ISBN 978-1-85418-369-9

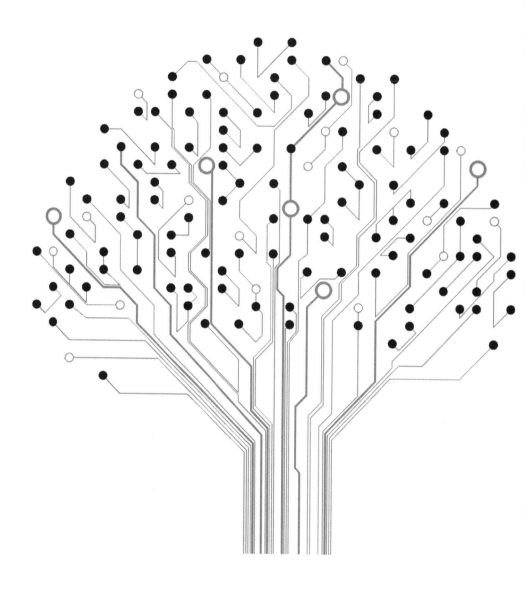

309

convergent thinking

WHAT IS IT?

Convergent thinking is a tool for problem solving in which the brain is applies a mechanized system or formula to some problem, where the solution is a number of steps from the problem. This kind of thinking is particularly appropriate in science, engineering, maths and technology.

Convergent thinking is opposite from divergent thinking in which a person generates many unique, creative responses to a single question or problem. Divergent thinking is followed by convergent thinking, in which a designer assesses, judges, and strengthens those options. Divergent thinking is what we do when we don't know the answer, when we don't know the next step

WHO INVENTED IT?

Hudson 1967,
Joy Paul Guilford

WHY USE THIS METHOD?

1. Convergent thinking leads to a single best answer, leaving no room for ambiguity.
2. Focuses on recognizing the familiar, reapplying techniques, and accumulating stored information

CHALLENGES

1. Divergent and convergent thinking need to be used together to solve many problems.
2. Designers and business managers are working on many problems which require divergent thinking due to changing complex environments.
3. Traditional management and engineering education stresses convergent thinking.

WHEN TO USE THIS METHOD

1. Explore Concepts
2. Make Plans

HOW TO USE THIS METHOD
Some of the rules of convergent thinking are:

1. Follow a systematic approach, find the patterns affinities and structure in a group of ideas.,
2. Use methods to evaluate ideas, assess qualitative and quantitative measures of ideas,
3. Avoid quickly ruling out an area of consideration, take your time.
4. Do not expend too much time in looking for the optimal solution of an ill-structured multi-criteria problem,
5. Assess risks and have a contingency plan.

REFERENCES

1. Cropley, Arthur (2006). "In Praise of Convergent Thinking". Creativity Research Journal 18: 391—404.

divergent thinking

WHAT IS IT?
The design process is a series of divergent and convergent phases. During the divergent phase of design the designer creates a number of choices. The goal of this approach is to analyze alternative approaches to test for the most stable solution. Divergent thinking is what we do when we don't know the answer, when we don't know the next step. Divergent thinking is followed by convergent thinking, in which a designer assesses, judges, and strengthens those options.

WHO INVENTED IT?
Hudson 1967,
Joy Paul Guilford

WHY USE THIS METHOD?
1. To an extent the number of choices created and compared during the divergent phases of design help determine the quality of the finished design.

CHALLENGES
1. Use when objectives are changing or ill defined.
1. Divergent and convergent thinking need to be used together to solve many problems.
2. Designers and business managers are working on many problems which require divergent thinking due to changing complex environments.

Image Copyright sippakorn, 2012
Used under license from Shutterstock.com

WHEN TO USE THIS METHOD
1. Frame insights
2. Explore Concepts
3. Make Plans

HOW TO USE THIS METHOD
Some of the rules for divergent thinking are:
1. Reframe the problem
2. See the problem from different perspectives,
3. Connect with and have empathy with the people that you are designing for.
4. Defer negative criticism.
5. Generate lots of ideas.
6. Combine and modify ideas,
7. Stretch the ideas, imagine ideas beyond normal limits,
8. Do not be afraid to break paradigms

RESOURCES
1. Pens
2. Paper
3. White board
4. Dry erase markers
5. Post it notes.

REFERENCES
1. Wade, Carole; Tavris, Carol (2008). Invitation to Psychology. Upper Saddle River, NJ: Pearson – Prentice Hall. pp. 258. ISBN 0-13-601609.

COUNTERMEASURES MATRIX

PROBLEM STATEMENT ....
....
....

CAUSES	COUNTERMEASURES	ACTIONS	IMPORTANCE	TOTAL	PRIORITY

countermeasures matrix

WHAT IS IT?
A countermeasures matrix documents a problem and identifies root causes, solutions and implementation priorities.

WHY USE THIS METHOD?
1. To identify next steps in the problem-solving process.
2. To document the team's findings and recommended actions.
3. To prioritize required resources for process improvement implementation activities.

WHEN TO USE THIS METHOD
1. Define intent
2. Know Context
3. Know User
4. Frame insights

HOW TO USE THIS METHOD
1. Create the problem statement and brainstorm a list of the root causes
2. For each cause, identify three things to do as countermeasures.
3. Rank the effectiveness of each countermeasure: one, two, three
4. Identify the specific actions to do it for each countermeasure.
5. Rank the feasibility in time and cost of each specific action : one, two, three
6. The moderator tabulates the ratings and indicates action priorities on the matrix.
7. Rate the action items on the basis of importance or feasibility to implement: one, two,three, four, five

RESOURCES
1. Pens
2. Paper
3. White board
4. Dry erase markers

creative problem solving process

WHAT IS IT?

It is a method for generating solutions to problems. Sometimes also known as the Osborn–Parnes CPS process.

WHO INVENTED IT?

Alex Osborn and Dr. Sidney J. Parnes in the 1950s

WHY USE THIS METHOD?

1. A flexible method
2. Uses both divergent and convergent thinking at each phase.

WHEN TO USE THIS METHOD

1. Define intent
2. Know Context
3. Know User
4. Frame insights
5. Explore Concepts
6. Make Plans
7. Deliver Offering

RESOURCES

1. Pens
2. Paper
3. Post it notes
4. White board
5. Dry erase markers
6. Video camera

HOW TO USE THIS METHOD

1. Each phase starts with generation of many alternative followed by a process of analysis and selection.

Explore the Challenge

1. Define your goal.
2. Research users stakeholders and context.
3. Problem Finding Identify the problem that need to be solved .

Generate Ideas

1. Brainstorm a list of ideas that solve the problem.

Prepare for Action

1. Solution Finding (move from idea to implementation solution)
2. Create plan for action)

REFERENCES

1. Hurson, Tim (2007). Think Better: An Innovator's Guide to Productive Thinking. New York, New York: McGraw Hill. pp. xii. ISBN 978-0-07-149493-9.

group circle

WHAT IS IT?

This is a way of positioning your team members to facilitate open communication, brainstorming and ideas sharing. It is the best arrangement of people to enable reading of body language. Non verbal communication represents more than 80% of communication between people. It is an approach widely used in schools and in traditional societies for meetings.

WHO INVENTED IT?

Part of UK school teaching pedagogy.

WHY USE THIS METHOD?

1. Helps democratic communication.
2. Shifts responsibility from moderator top participants.

CHALLENGES

1. Communication is best without a table. A table may be necessary for some intended activities

WHEN TO USE THIS METHOD

2. Frame insights
3. Explore Concepts
4. Make Plans

HOW TO USE THIS METHOD

1. Between 5 and 20 people is the optimum number of participants.
2. Participants sit in a circle on chairs or around a circular table or on the floor on cushions.
3. Can pass around an object and when the person holds the object they can speak and the other participants listen

RESOURCES

1. Table
2. Chairs or cushions
3. White board
4. Dry erase markers
5. Paper
6. Pens

REFERENCES

1. Mosley, J. and Tew, M. (1999) Quality Circle Time in the Secondary School – A Handbook of Good Practice. David Fulton Publishers: London
2. Lloyd, G. and Munn, P. (eds) (1998) Sharing Good Practice: Prevention and Support for Pupils with Social, Emotional and Behavioral Difficulties. Moray House Publications: Edinburgh

DOUBLE REVERSAL PROCESS

1

PREVIOUSLY BRAINSTORMED IDEAS

2

REVERSE THE PROBLEM
BRAINSTORM NEW IDEAS

3

REVERSE THE REVERSED
PROBLEM IDEAS

4

ADD NEW IDEAS TO PREVIOUSLY
BRAINSTORMED IDEAS

double reversal

WHAT IS IT?

The double reversal is a type of brainstorming that can be used when a team has tried other techniques with limited success. The problem is first reversed and ideas are generated then each idea is reversed to gain a new perspective on the problem.

WHY USE THIS METHOD?

1. To identify new solutions for a design problem.
1. To expand a list of previously brainstormed ideas.
1. To take a new perspective after an unproductive brainstorming effort.

WHEN TO USE THIS METHOD

1. Explore Concepts

HOW TO USE THIS METHOD

1. Start with a collection of previously brainstormed ideas.
2. Display the ideas and discuss them with your team.
3. Reverse the objective.
4. Your team brainstorms how to make the problem worse with each idea.
5. Record the ideas on a white board the double reversal process.
6. The team reverses the ideas. A double reversal.
7. Add the new set of ideas to the original set.

RESOURCES

1. Pens
2. Paper
3. White board
4. Dry erase markers
5. Post it notes.

gunning fog index

WHAT IS IT?

The gunning fog index is an index of the reading level required to understand written information. The fog index allows a designer to know whether written material can be understood by a target reading audience and to make adjustments if necessary.

WHO INVENTED IT?

Robert Gunning, 1952

WHY USE THIS METHOD?

1. To determine a reading level requirement for one's writing.
2. To estimate an educational level needed to understand written information.
3. The fog index is used to understand what level of text can be most easily read by a particular audience,

RESOURCES

1. Pen
2. Paper

REFERENCES

1. Gunning, R. (1952). The technique of clear writing. New York, NY: McGraw-Hill International Book Co.

WHEN TO USE THIS METHOD

1. Know Context
2. Know User
3. Frame insights

HOW TO USE THIS METHOD

The Gunning fog index is calculated in the following way:

1. Select a passage of one or more full paragraphs of around 100 words.
2. Do not leave out any sentences.
3. Calculate the average sentence length. by dividing the number of words by the number of sentences.
4. Count the "complex" words: those with three or more syllables.
5. Do not include proper nouns, jargon, or compound words. Do not include common suffixes such as –es, –ed, or –ing as a syllable;
6. Add the average sentence length and the percentage of complex words
7. Multiply the result by 0.4.
8. Texts for a wide audience generally need a fog index less than 12.
9. Texts requiring universal understanding need an index less than 8.
10. A U.S. high school senior around 18 years old should have a fog index of around 12.

OBJECTS

remote control
button
computer
phone
car
sailboat
camera
television
internet
gps
mp3 player
book

ACTIONS

smell
hear
touch
see
walk
sing
talk
dance
vision
laugh
magic
swim
play
tell a story

heuristic ideation

WHAT IS IT?

Heuristic ideation method is used to create new concepts, ideas, products or solutions.

WHY USE THIS METHOD?

1. To create new connections and insights for products, services and experiences

WHO INVENTED IT?

Couger 1995, McFadzean 1998, McFadzean, Somersall, and Coker 1998, VanGundy 1988

RESOURCES

1. Pens
2. Markers
3. White board or flip chart
4. Dry erase markers

WHEN TO USE THIS METHOD

1. Explore Concepts

HOW TO USE THIS METHOD

1. The group will first make two lists of words
2. Each team member selects three words from the first list and connects each word to a different word in the second list.
3. Each team members develops these ideas into concepts and illustrates or describes each concept on an index card.
4. The index cards are places on a pin board and each concept is briefly described by the team member who generated the idea.
5. The team votes to prioritize the ideas

REFERENCES

1. McFadzean, E. Creativity in MS / OR: Choosing the Appropriate Technique — Interfaces 29: 5 September — October 1999 (pp 110 — 122)

idea advocate

WHAT IS IT?

This method involves appointing advocates for ideas that were previously created during a brainstorming session.

WHO INVENTED IT?

Battelle Institute in Frankfurt, Germany

WHY USE THIS METHOD?

1. Idea advocate is a simplified form of the dialectical approach
2. To ensure fair examination of all ideas.
3. To give every presented idea equal chance of being selected.
4. To uncover the positive aspects of ideas

CHALLENGES

1. Consideration should be given to also assigning a devil's advocate for a more balanced assessment of certain proposed ideas.
2. There should be little difference in status amongst the idea advocates.

WHEN TO USE THIS METHOD

1. Explore Concepts

HOW TO USE THIS METHOD

1. The team reviews a list of previously generated ideas.
2. Assign idea advocate roles to:
3. A team member who proposed an idea, will implement an idea, or argues for the selection of a design direction.
4. The idea advocates present arguments to the design team on why the idea is the best direction.
5. After the advocates have presented the team votes on their preferred idea.

RESOURCES

1. Pens
2. Markers
3. White board or flip chart
4. Dry erase markers

information market

WHAT IS IT?

A method of exploring a problem involving hundreds of participants and a large space. This method has been used for community planning activities.

WHO INVENTED IT?

Metaplan GmbH 1970s

WHY USE THIS METHOD?

1. Lower participation costs.

CHALLENGES

1. Involves considerable pre planning.

WHEN TO USE THIS METHOD

1. Define intent
2. Know Context
3. Know User
4. Frame insights
5. Explore Concepts

HOW TO USE THIS METHOD

1. A large space
2. 600 to 1000 participants
3. Arrange 10 to 20 booths around the space
4. Each booth has three number of trained moderators'
5. Each booth explores a question.
6. Participants can select the booths they would like to participate in.
7. Participants vote on outcomes of discussion topics.

RESOURCES

1. White boards
2. Dry erase markers
3. Tents or booths
4. Chairs

REFERENCES

1. Linde, Frank and Stock, Wolfgang G. (2011). Information Markets. A Strategic Guideline for the I-Commerce. Berlin, New York, New York: De Gruyter Saur.

matchett's
fundamental design method

WHAT IS IT?

Matchett's Fundamental Design Method is an approach to developing and applying design strategies.

Edward Matchett (1929—1998) worked as a design engineer in a number of respected research and development offices in the UK including Rolls Royce. From 1966 to 1970, he researched the creative process, for the Science Research Council of Great Britain.

The aim of this research was to find methods of improving "creativeness, professionalism and achievement" in product design and development. From 1958 Matchett developed his Fundamental Design Method (FDM). Matchett believed that "the most advanced form of FDM lifts a mind into 'meta-control', making it possible to produce the quality and quantity of thoughts and actions that are normally produced only by a person of genius."

"Anyone wishing to try out FDM without the help of it's inventor should recognize that he is exploring the part of experience that is accessible through religion, through art, through psycho-analysis, through group dynamics, through drug-taking, through insanity, through self mastery courses and through indoctrination: it is an aspect of experience that some people believe to be wickedness or self delusion and others believe to be the ultimate reality and the ultimate good."
Quote from John Chris Jones Design Methods.

WHO INVENTED IT?

Edward Matchett and Briggs 1966

WHY USE THIS METHOD?

1. It has been applied successfully by many UK companies and is a product of it's inventor and of the 1960s culture.

CHALLENGES

1. See quote above *John Chris Jones*

WHEN TO USE THIS METHOD

1. Define intent
2. Know Context
3. Know User
4. Frame insights
5. Explore Concepts

HOW TO USE THIS METHOD

1. Undergo training in FDM. The content and complexity of the method is beyond the scope of this publication.
2. After training apply the following modes of thinking
   ◦ Thinking with outline strategies
   ◦ Thinking in parallel planes
   ◦ Thinking from several viewpoints
   ◦ Thinking with concepts
   ◦ Thinking with basic elements.
3. Use the FDM design sequence and checklists.

RESOURCES

The Matchett Foundation,
14 Montrose Avenue,
Redland,
Bristol BS6 6EQ

REFERENCES

4. Jones, John Christopher. Design Methods. 1992. Wiley. ISBN 0-471-28496-3.

MORPHOLOGICAL CHART

PRODUCT	TYPE	SIZE	STYLE	FINISH	MATERIAL

morphological analysis

WHAT IS IT?
This is a method that helps to generate concepts by combining components of a design in a new arrangement.

WHO INVENTED IT?
Fritz Zwicky Caltech 1966
Norris, K.W. 1963

WHY USE THIS METHOD?
1. To help expand the possible solutions to a design problem.

RESOURCES
1. Pen
2. Paper
3. White board
4. Dry erase markers
5. Post-it-notes

WHEN TO USE THIS METHOD
1. Explore Concepts

HOW TO USE THIS METHOD
1. Define your design problem
2. Define the attributes of the design solution.
3. Create a matrix
4. List each component of the design as a column heading on the top horizontal axis of the matrix
5. Write down or illustrate as many variations of each component as possible in the column below the attribute
6. Select one component from each column and combine them into a new concept.
7. This can be done by intuition or randomly.
8. Develop the best ideas.

REFERENCES
1. Bailey, K.(1994) Typologies and Taxonomies – An Introduction to Classification Techniques, Sage University Papers: Thousand Oaks.
2. Bailey, K.(1994) Typologies and Taxonomies – An Introduction to Classification Techniques, Sage University Papers: Thousand Oaks.

page's strategy

WHAT IS IT?
The aim of this method is to reduce the time spent developing unsuccessful design directions.

WHO INVENTED IT?
J.K. Page 1963

WHY USE THIS METHOD?
1. The strategy aims to reduce trial and error in the design process.
2. In a usual design process much time is unproductive due to oversights.

WHEN TO USE THIS METHOD
1. Explore Concepts

HOW TO USE THIS METHOD
1. Define goals
2. Define external factors that may prevent a design from achieving the goals.
3. Define tests for unacceptable solutions.
4. Brainstorm a wide range of design ideas.
5. Analyze the design ideas to determine which pass or fail the tests.
6. Combine solutions to eliminate conflicts.
7. Prioritize the solutions

RESOURCES
1. White board
2. Dry erase markers
3. Pens
4. Paper

pattern language

WHAT IS IT?

Pattern language is an approach to design that uses visual icons rather than words to stimulate and develop design concepts. Developed by Alexander to discover the design factors such as life, wholeness or spirit for architectural projects that he called design elements that give a community "the quality that has no name"

WHO INVENTED IT?

Christopher Alexander, Sara Ishikawa, Murray Silverstein 1977

WHY USE THIS METHOD?

1. A non verbal approach to design.

RESOURCES

1. Blank Index cards
2. Pens
3. Paper

WHEN TO USE THIS METHOD

1. Explore Concepts

HOW TO USE THIS METHOD

1. Write a list of about 250 words that are attributes or factors of your design problem.
2. Create a series of iconic images to illustrate each word on a deck of blank index cards.
3. Write the associated word on the back face of each icon card.
4. Spread the cards on a table with the icons facing upwards and randomly associate two or three cards at a time.
5. Generate concepts based on these associations.
6. Review the ideas with your team
7. Prioritize the ideas.
8. Develop preferred ideas.

REFERENCES

1. Alexander, C., Ishikawa, S., Silverstein, Murray. (1977). A pattern language. New York: Oxford University Press.

pearson's method

WHAT IS IT?

Pearson's note book method is a method of generating ideas for products, services and experiences using a team of people in different locations. The idea generation takes place over a three week period.

WHO INVENTED IT?

Pearson 1979

WHY USE THIS METHOD?

1. The extended period allows deeper exploration of ideas through incubation.

CHALLENGES

1. Requires time
2. Can involve a lot of work to coordinate

WHEN TO USE THIS METHOD

1. Explore Concepts

RESOURCES

2. Pens
3. Note pad
4. Cameras

HOW TO USE THIS METHOD

1. Participants are selected form a number of organizations in different geographical locations.
2. Each participant is given a notebook and a scenario to explore.
3. Each participant records one idea on one page in a notebook for two weeks.
4. Each participant swaps their notebook with another participant and reviews the other participant's ideas
5. The participants continue for one more week to record one idea per day.
6. Experts give each participant more information at regular intervals over the one month period.
7. At the end of the one month period each participant selects their best idea and summarizes their thoughts.
8. The notebooks are collected.
9. The notebooks are reviewed by three coordinators and a summary of their contents is made.
10. Responses are organized into categories and recorded on index cards
11. Participants are shown the summary document.
12. A group discussion is organized and conducted with all of the participants and the design team and stakeholders.
13. The scenarios are compared and discussed to generate further ideas

phillips 66 method

WHAT IS IT?

The Phillips 66 method is a method for stimulating interaction such as questions, ideas, or opinions from a large conference group.

WHO INVENTED IT?

Donald Phillips

WHY USE THIS METHOD?

1. Involves a large number of people in a process to share ideas.
2. May generate a large number of ideas.

CHALLENGES

1. The original Phillips 66 process called for the dividing of a large group into groups of 6 people each and to allow 6 minutes per small group for discussing a problem or generating ideas.
2. The small group size should be adjusted to suite the size of the larger group and the discussion time should be adjusted to suite the problem being addressed
3. Two or more teams will generate the same idea through different methods of reasoning.

WHEN TO USE THIS METHOD

1. Explore Concepts

HOW TO USE THIS METHOD

1. Divide the larger group into smaller groups of between 4 and 8 people.
2. The moderator presents a clearly defined problem to all of the groups.
3. Each smaller group should move to an area where they can discuss the problem.
4. Each small group should select a spokesperson to record and later present their conclusions.
5. Each group should discuss the problem for between 6 and 30 minutes.
6. The group spokesperson records the ideas.
7. Each group selects the top one to three ideas. The number selected depends on time available for the presentations to the larger group.
8. The selected ideas are recorded and passed on to the moderator. This can be done using index cards.
9. The selected ideas are reviewed by the moderator and discussed by the larger group or reviewed and discussed at a later time.

RESOURCES

1. Pens
2. Index cards
3. Post-it-notes
4. White board
5. Dry erase markers.

productive thinking model

WHAT IS IT?

This method is an approach to solving problems based in part on "The creative problem solving process."

WHO INVENTED IT?

Tim Hurson

WHY USE THIS METHOD?

1. A flexible method
2. Uses both divergent and convergent thinking at each phase.

WHEN TO USE THIS METHOD

1. Define intent
2. Know Context
3. Know User
4. Frame insights
5. Explore Concepts

RESOURCES

1. Pens
2. Paper
3. Post it notes
4. White board
5. Dry erase markers
6. Video camera

REFERENCES

1. Hurson, Tim (2007). Think Better: An Innovator's Guide to Productive Thinking. New York, New York: McGraw Hill. pp. xii. ISBN 978-0-07-149493-9.

HOW TO USE THIS METHOD

Step 1: What's Going On?

1. Explores the context of the problem
2. What's the Itch? Brainstorm a list of problems or opportunities, to select one key problem to address
3. What's the Impact?
4. What's the Information?
5. Who's Involved? Identify stakeholders
6. What's the Vision?, Identify the desired effect of the design

Step 2: What's Success?

1. Establishes a vision for a future if the problem is solved
2. Do. What do you want the solution to do?
3. Restrictions. What must the solution not do?
4. Investment. What resources can be invested?
5. Values. What are the desired values?
6. Essential outcomes

Step 3: What's the Question?

1. Turns the goal into a question. "How might we.?"
2. Brainstorm questions
3. Select the best question to answer with the design.

Step 4: Generate Answers

1. Brainstorm a wide range of solutions and select the desired design direction for further development.

Step 5: Forge the Solution

1. Positives. What works?
2. Objections . What doesn't work?
3. What else? What does it remind you of?
4. Enhancements. How can the design be improved?
5. Remedies. How can conflicts be corrected?

Step 6: Align Resources

1. Create action plan
2. Create to do lists
3. Create time lines and milestones
4. Create list of stakeholders
5. Create list of issues that need further work

Source: [1]

REFRAMING MATRIX

PRODUCT PERSPECTIVE

1. Is there something wrong with the product or service?
2. Is it priced correctly?
3. How well does it serve the market?
4. Is it reliable?

PLANNING PERSPECTIVE

1. Are our business plans, marketing plans, or strategy at fault?
2. Could we improve these?

POTENTIAL PERSPECTIVE

1. How would we increase sales?
2. If we were to seriously increase our targets or our production volumes, what would happen with this problem?

PEOPLE PERSPECTIVE

1. What are the people impacts and people implications of the problem?
2. What do people involved with the problem think?
3. Why are customers not using or buying the product?

DESIGN PROBLEM . . . .

. . . .

reframing matrix

WHAT IS IT?
The reframing matrix is a method of approaching a problem by imagining the perspectives of a number of different people and exploring the possible solutions that they might suggest.

WHO INVENTED IT?
Michael Morgan 1993

WHY USE THIS METHOD?
1. This is a method for assisting in empathy which is an important factor in gaining acceptance and creating successful design.

CHALLENGES
1. The reframing is not done with stakeholders present or in context so may be subjective

RESOURCES
1. Pens
2. Paper
3. Post it notes
4. White board
5. Dry erase markers

WHEN TO USE THIS METHOD
1. Define intent

HOW TO USE THIS METHOD
1. Define a problem.
2. On a white board or paper draw a large square and divide it into four quadrants.
3. Select 4 different perspectives to approach the problem. They could be four professions or four people or four other perspectives that are important for your problem.
4. With your team brainstorm a number of questions that you believe are important from the perspectives that you have selected.
5. The moderator writes the questions in the relevant quadrants of the matrix.
6. The group discusses each of these questions.
7. The answers are recorded and the perspectives are incorporated into the considerations for design solutions.

REFERENCES
1. Morgan, M. Creating Workforce Innovation: Turning Individual Creativity into Organizational Innovation. Publisher: Business & Professional Pub (October 1993) ISBN-10: 1875680020 ISBN-13: 978-1875680023

rich pictures

WHAT IS IT?

Rich Pictures is a method for learning about complex or ill-defined problems by asking participants to draw detailed pictures of them and to explain the drawings.

WHO INVENTED IT?

Rich pictures originated in Soft Systems Methodologies developed during the 1960s and 1970s by Peter Checkland and students at Lancaster University

WHY USE THIS METHOD?

1. This is a method for assisting in empathy which is an important factor in gaining acceptance and creating successful design.

REFERENCES

1. Monk, A. F. Lightweight techniques to encourage innovative user interface design. In L. Wood & R. Zeno, eds., Bridging the Gap: Transforming User Requirements into User Interface Design. CRC Press,Boca Raton, 1997.

2. Avison, D. and Fitzgerald, G. Information Systems Development: Methodologies, Techniques and Tools. Blackwell Scientific Publishers, Oxford,1988.

WHEN TO USE THIS METHOD

1. Know Context
2. Know User
3. Frame insights

HOW TO USE THIS METHOD

1. The moderator asks each participant to draw two pictures.
2. Ask the participants to draw a picture of how they want to see a situation, activity, product, service or experience in the future.
3. Ask the participants to draw a second picture of how they see the current situation, activity, product, service or experience.
4. Each participant explains first the picture of the present situation;
5. Ask the participants to explain what, when, where, how and why for each picture.
6. Brainstorm ideas to move from the present to the future.

RESOURCES

1. Pens
2. Paper
3. Digital voice recorder
4. Camera
5. Video camera.

secret voting

WHAT IS IT?

This method is an approach to selecting preferred ideas for further development.

WHY USE THIS METHOD?

1. Protects participants from interpersonal pressures when selecting preferred ideas,
2. Results in more democratic selection of ideas.

CHALLENGES

1. Complete anonymity is hard to achieve.

WHEN TO USE THIS METHOD

1. Frame insights
2. Explore Concepts

HOW TO USE THIS METHOD

1. The design team generates a range of concepts. Such as 100 ideas
2. This can be the output of a day's work individually sketching based on a design brief.
3. Each idea is numbered and the ideas are pinned on a large pin board.
4. The ideas are explained by the creator of each idea in a short presentation to the group.
5. The moderator hands out five index cards to each participant.
6. Each participant votes for their preferred designs assigning five points for their favorite idea and four points for their next preferred idea.
7. The cards are handed face down to the moderator who totals the votes.
8. The three designs with the highest points are selected for further development.
9. Participants cannot vote for their own ideas.

SIMPLEX METHOD

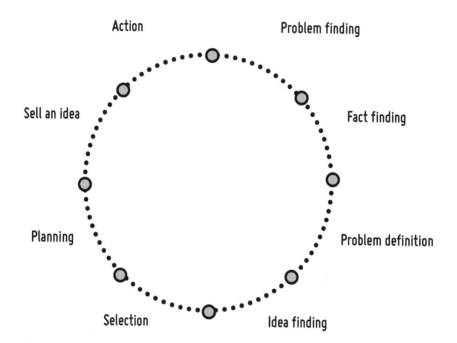

simplex method

WHAT IS IT?
Simplex is a method that uses both analytical and creative thinking in a team-based approach and can be applied through the full design process.

WHO INVENTED IT?
Min Basadur, 1994

WHY USE THIS METHOD?
1. A flexible method
2. Uses both divergent and convergent thinking at each phase.
3. It is suitable for small and large scale problems and projects.
1. Problems uncovered by the Simplex system should be addressed, starting at step one, as part of a continuous improvement effort.

WHEN TO USE THIS METHOD
1. Define intent
2. Know Context
3. Know User
4. Frame insights
5. Explore Concepts

RESOURCES
1. Pens
2. Paper
3. Post it notes
4. White board
5. Dry erase markers
6. Video camera

HOW TO USE THIS METHOD
1. **Find the problem**
   - Customers needs and desires
   - What are our core competencies?
   - What are our problems?
   - How can we improve quality?
   - What are our competitors doing?
   - What is frustrating our team?
2. **Find the facts**
   - How do others perceive the situation?
   - Analyze data.
   - Look at your competitor's good ideas.
   - Understand customers.
   - Look at what has been tried.
   - What are the services that are possible?
   - What are the technologies and processes that are possible?
   - Is there good return on investment?
3. **Define the problem you should solve.**
4. **Brainstorm the best idea.**
5. **Evaluating and select solution**
6. **Plan action**
7. **Sell the idea.**
8. **Take action**

REFERENCES
1. Basadur, Min. The Power of Innovation: How to Make Innovation a Way of Life & How to Put Creative Solutions to Work. June 1, 1995. Financial Times/Prentice Hall. ISBN-10: 0273613626 ISBN-13: 978-0273613626

small groups

WHAT IS IT?

The optimum group size for creativity is 4 or five people. A large group can be broken down into smaller groups to optimize creative output.

WHY USE THIS METHOD?

1. To optimize creative output.
2. To save time by having parallel discussions.
3. To minimize groupthink

WHEN TO USE THIS METHOD

1. Define intent
2. Know Context
3. Know User
4. Frame insights
5. Explore Concepts
6. Make Plans
7. Deliver Offering

HOW TO USE THIS METHOD

1. If you have a large group break the group down into smaller groups of 4 or 5 people.
2. The moderator asks the smaller groups to consider the problem or generate ideas.
3. Each member of the smaller groups can generate a number of ideas or solutions.
4. Each participant in each small group presents each idea to the small group.
5. The small group votes internally for their top two or three ideas and selects a spokesperson.
6. The spokesperson presents the top two or three ideas to the larger group.
7. The larger group votes for the preferred ideas overall.

sociodrama

WHAT IS IT?

Sociodrama is concerned with social learning and problem solving in a group by dramatic methods. Actors play out everyday experiences and interact with an audience. The method is used in institutions such as police academies for training.

WHO INVENTED IT?

Jacob L. Moreno 1910

WHY USE THIS METHOD?

1. Used in business, education, and professional training

WHEN TO USE THIS METHOD

1. Know Context
2. Know User
3. Explore Concepts

REFERENCES

1. Kellermann, P. (2007) Sociodrama and Collective Trauma.
2. B. Clark, J. Burmeister, and M. Maciel, "Psychodrama: Advances in Theory and Practice." (2007) Taylor and Frances: USA. ISBN 0-415-41914-X
3. The workbook. A guide to the development and presentation of issue oriented, audience interactive, improvisational theatre. New York: Taylor & Francis Group. Dayton, T. (1990). Drama games. Techniques for self development.

HOW TO USE THIS METHOD

1. The actors are briefed in their roles, and characters motivations, expected behavior in the scene.
2. The activity may take place on a stage.
3. A common approach is to use a volunteer chosen from the of participants being trained who is given a role to perform.
4. The moderator will ask the actor to stop and then ask the audience for critical feedback of the scene. This method relies on dialogue with the audience. The dialogue should occur in a neutral manner.
5. The moderator steers the dialogue which is the tool for education and conscience raising.

RESOURCES

1. Stage or theater
2. Props
3. Costumes
4. Video camera

strategy switching

WHAT IS IT?

The aim of this method is to find the best balance of a strategy which is neither too rigid nor too flexible and to balance planned and unplanned thinking or analytical and creative thinking.

WHO INVENTED IT?

Broadbent 1966
Jones 1963
Mann 1963

WHY USE THIS METHOD?

1. Low cost
2. Does not take much time
3. Helps speed projects by avoiding haphazard strategy changes.
4. Can be applied to team or individual projects.

CHALLENGES

1. Requires ability to think on two modes of thought simultaneously.

WHEN TO USE THIS METHOD

1. Define intent
2. Know Context
3. Know User
4. Frame insights
5. Explore Concepts

HOW TO USE THIS METHOD

1. Brainstorm strategies
2. Select preferred strategy
3. While developing strategy over project compile a list of spontaneous thoughts regarding alternative strategies suggested by team members
4. At several points during project review alternative strategies.
5. When an alternative strategy appears to be viable develop a second design project using the alternative strategy.
6. Review progress of the two design developments and either retain original strategy or cease original strategy and switch to alternative strategy
7. Repeat above process as necessary.

RESOURCES

1. Paper
2. Pens
3. White board
4. Dry erase markers
5. Post-it-notes

vroom yetton decision model

WHAT IS IT?

This method assists in the selection of a leadership style for group decision making.

This model identifies five different styles They are:

1. Autocratic Type 1 (AI) — Leader makes own decision .
2. Autocratic Type 2 (AII) — Leader collects required information from followers, then makes decision alone.
3. Consultative Type 1 (CI) — Leader shares problem to relevant followers individually and seeks their ideas & suggestions and makes decision alone.
4. Consultative Type 2 (CII) — Leader shares problem to relevant followers as a group and seeks their ideas & suggestions and makes decision alone. Here followers' meet each other and through discussions they understand other alternatives.
5. Group-based Type 2(GII) — Leader discuss problem & situation with followers as a group and seeks their ideas & suggestions through brainstorming. Leader accepts any decision & do not try to force his idea. Decision accepted by the group is the final one.

Source: Vroom, V. H. & Jago, A. G.

HOW TO USE THIS METHOD

Vroom & Yetton formulated following seven questions on decision quality. Answer to the following questions must be either 'Yes' or 'No' with the current scenario.

1. Is there a quality requirement? Is the nature of the solution critical? Are there technical or rational grounds for selecting among possible solutions?
2. Do I have sufficient information to make a high quality decision?
3. Is the problem structured? Are the alternative courses of action and methods for their evaluation known?
4. Is acceptance of the decision by subordinates critical to its implementation?
5. If I were to make the decision by myself, is it reasonably certain that it would be accepted by my subordinates?
6. Do subordinates share the organizational goals to be obtained in solving this problem?
7. Is conflict among subordinates likely in obtaining the preferred solution?
8. Based on the answers one can find out the styles from the graph.

Source: Vroom, V. H. & Jago, A. G.

Vroom & Yetton, and later Vroom & Jago found the following questions helpful in the sequence below:

1. Quality Requirement (QR): How important is the technical quality of the decision?
2. Commitment Requirement (CR): How important is subordinate commitment to the decision?
3. Leader's Information (LI): Do you (the leader) have sufficient information to make a high quality decision on your own?
4. Problem Structure (ST): Is the problem well structured (e.g., defined, clear, organized, lend itself to solution, time limited, etc.)?
5. Commitment Probability (CP): If you were to make the decision by yourself, is it reasonably certain that your subordinates would be committed to the decision?
6. Goal Congruence (GC): Do subordinates share the organizational goals to be attained in solving the problem?
7. Subordinate conflict (CO): Is conflict among subordinates over preferred solutions likely?
8. Subordinate information (SI): Do subordinates have sufficient information to make a high quality decision?

Source: Vroom, V. H. & Jago, A. G.

WHEN TO USE THIS METHOD

1. Frame insights
2. Explore Concepts

WHO INVENTED IT?

Victor Vroom, Phillip Yetton 1973

WHY USE THIS METHOD?

1. Taking people off their primary tasks to participate in teams or other decision making activities may be good empowerment, but when unnecessary it can be costly.
2. The Vroom-Yetton-Jago model is a decision making tree that enables a leader to examine a situation and determine which style or level of involvement to engage

REFERENCES

1. Vroom, Victor H.; Yetton, Phillip W. (1973). Leadership and Decision-Making. Pittsburgh: University of Pittsburgh Press. ISBN 0-8229-3266-0.
2. Vroom, Victor H.; Jago, Arthur G. (1988). The New Leadership: Managing Participation in Organizations. Englewood Cliffs, NJ: Prentice-Hall. ISBN 0-13-615030-6.
3. Vroom, Victor; Sternberg, Robert J. (2002). "Theoretical Letters: The person versus the situation in leadership". The Leadership Quarterly 13: 301—323. doi:10.1016/S1048-9843(02)00101-7.

WORD DIAMOND

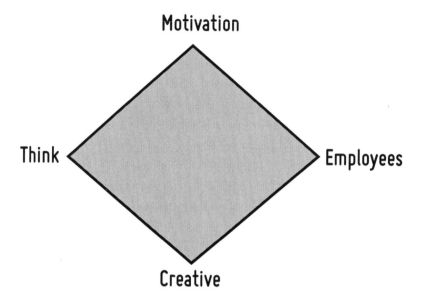

Source: Elspeth McFadzean

word diamond

WHAT IS IT?
Word Diamond is a technique developed in order to generate ideas from the problem statement.

WHO INVENTED IT?
VanGundy 1992

WHY USE THIS METHOD?
1. This exercise can be performed by anyone.
2. Does not require an experienced group or moderator.

RESOURCES
1. Paper
2. Pens
3. White board
4. Dry erase markers
5. Post-it-notes

REFERENCES
1. Encouraging Creative Thinking Author: Elspeth McFadzean, Henley Management College, Henley-on-Thames, UK First published: 2000

WHEN TO USE THIS METHOD
1. Define intent
2. Frame insights
3. Explore Concepts

HOW TO USE THIS METHOD

1. "The group participants choose four words or phrases from the problem statement.
2. These words can then be placed in a diamond shape so that each word or phrase lies at one of the points.
3. The group participants are asked to combine the words or phrases together and to tell the facilitator the ideas that have occurred due to the combination. The facilitator writes the ideas down on a flip chart.
4. Next, the two words, which were initially selected, are combined with a third word to develop more ideas.
5. Steps 3 and 4 are repeated until all possible combinations are examined and all the ideas have been recorded.
6. The group continues to combine words and record ideas until they have exhausted all possibilities. These ideas can then be analyzed and developed into workable solutions"

Source: VanGundy 1992

Chapter 7
Prototype and iterate
how can we make it better?

a/b testing

WHAT IS IT?
A/B testing is a method of testing two versions of a design in order to find out which version people respond to in the most positive way. Different users prefer different designs. It is also called split testing.

WHO INVENTED IT?
Karl Pearson,1900
A/B testing has been used by companies such as Amazon, Google, Microsoft and the BBC.

WHY USE THIS METHOD?
1. Helps to identify the best combination of elements to contribute to a successful design.

CHALLENGES
1. It may take some time to get sufficient data.
2. Not as effective as talking to users or usability tests
3. Increased certainty needs a larger sample

WHEN TO USE THIS METHOD
1. Know Context
2. Know User
3. Frame insights
4. Explore Concepts

HOW TO USE THIS METHOD
1. Develop two versions of a design
2. Randomly divide users into two groups
3. Show each group a different version
4. Track how users perform
5. Evaluate using statistical analysis.
6. Develop the more successful design

An example of a/b testing for an e-mail campaign.
1. Send 1,000 e-mails to a user group with one response code
2. Send 1,000 e-mails to a different user group with a different response code
3. Vary details such as the subject line, layout, images, colors, wording of each e-mail.
4. Compare the response rate for each e-mail.

REFERENCES
1. Kohavi, R.; Longbotham, R., Sommerfield, D., Henne, R.M. (2009). Controlled experiments on the web: survey and practical guide. Data Mining and Knowledge Discovery (Berlin: Springer) 18 (1): 140—181. doi:10.1007/s10618-008-0114-1. ISSN 1384-5810.

generative prototyping

WHAT IS IT?
A method also called "Thinkering" where participants build simple prototypes from supplied materials to explore ideas.

WHO INVENTED IT?
Pioneered by Liz Sanders 2002 and Lego Johan Roos and Bart Victor 1990s.

WHY USE THIS METHOD?
1. Creative way to generate ideas involving users
2. Discovering user needs
3. Developing concepts with users
4. Designing prototypes with users

CHALLENGES
1. Demanding of participants:
2. Good moderation needed
1. Designers can become too attached to their prototypes and allow them to become jewelry that stands in the way of further refinement.

WHEN TO USE THIS METHOD
1. Know Context
2. Know User
3. Frame insights
4. Explore Concepts

HOW TO USE THIS METHOD
1. "In generative prototyping users are asked to together with designers built low-tech prototypes or products using a large set of materials during a workshop. For example, in creating ideas for a new playground, children were asked to built their favorite playground element using ice lolly sticks, foam balls, etc
2. The basic idea is that by building, you start thinking and new ideas are generated."
source: Geke Luken

RESOURCES
1. Toy construction kits such as lego
2. Pop sticks
3. String
4. Tape
5. Post-it-notes
6. Cardboard
7. Paper
8. Markers

REFERENCES
1. Statler, M., Roos, J., and B. Victor, 2009, 'Ain't Misbehavin': Taking Play Seriously in Organizations,' Journal of Change Management, 9(1): 87-107.

dark horse prototype

WHAT IS IT?
A dark horse prototype is your most creative idea built as a fast prototype. The innovative approach serves as a focus for finding the optimum real solution to the design problem.

WHO INVENTED IT?
One of the methods taught at Stanford University.

WHY USE THIS METHOD?
1. This method is a way of breaking free of average solutions and exploring unknown territory
2. A way of challenging assumptions.

CHALLENGES
1. Fear of unexplored directions
2. Fear of change
1. Designers can become too attached to their prototypes and allow them to become jewelry that stands in the way of further refinement.
2. Client may believe that system is real.

WHEN TO USE THIS METHOD
1. Explore Concepts

HOW TO USE THIS METHOD
1. After initial brainstorming sessions select with your team the most challenging, interestingly or thought provoking idea.
2. Create a low resolution prototype of the selected idea.
3. With your team analyze and discuss the prototype.
4. Brainstorm ways of bringing back the dark horse concept into a realizable solution.

REFERENCES
1. Constantine, L. L., Windl, H., Noble, J., and Lockwood, L. A. D. "From Abstraction to Realization in User Interface Design: Abstract Prototypes Based on Canonical Components." Working Paper, The Convergence Colloquy, July 2000.

pictive

1. WHAT IS IT?

PICTIVE (Plastic Interface for Collaborative Technology Initiative through Video Exploration) is a low fidelity participatory design method used to develop graphical user interfaces. It allows users to participate in the development process. A PICTIVE prototype gives a user a sense of what a system or a piece of software will look like and how it will behave when completed.

WHO INVENTED IT?

Developed by Michael J. Muller and others at Bell Communications Research around 1990

WHY USE THIS METHOD?

2. Less development time.
3. Less development costs.
4. Involves users.
5. Gives quantifiable user feedback.
6. Facilitates system implementation since users know what to expect.
7. Results user oriented solutions.
8. Gets users with diverse experience involved.

CHALLENGES

1. Designers can become too attached to their prototypes and allow them to become jewelry that stands in the way of further refinement.
2. Don't worry about it being pretty.

WHEN TO USE THIS METHOD

1. Explore Concepts

HOW TO USE THIS METHOD

1. A PICTIVE is usually made from simple available tools and materials like pens, paper, Post-It stickers, paper clips and icons on cards.
2. Allow thirty minutes for initial design.
3. Allow ten minutes for user testing.
4. Ten minutes for modification.
5. Five minutes for user testing.
6. Create task scenario.
7. Anything that moves or changes should be a separate element.
8. The designer uses these materials to represent elements such as drop-down boxes, menu bars, and special icons. During a design session, users modify the mock up based on their own experience.
9. Take notes for later review.
10. Record the session with a video camera
11. The team then reviews the ideas and develops a strategy to apply them.
12. A PICTIVE enables non technical people to participate in the design process.

REFERENCES

1. Michael J. Muller PICTIVE an exploration in participatory design. Published in: Proceeding CHI '91 Proceedings of the SIGCHI Conference on Human Factors in Computing Systems Pages 225-231 ACM New York, NY, USA ©1991 table of contents ISBN:0-89791-383-3 doi 10.1145/108844.108896

appearance prototype

WHAT IS IT?

Appearance prototypes look like but do not work like the final product. The are often fabricated using a variety of rapid prototyping techniques from digital 3d models or by hand in materials such as hard foam, wood or plastics. Usually, appearance prototypes are "for show" and short term use and are not designed to be handled.

CHALLENGES

1. Designers can become too attached to their prototypes and allow them to become jewelry that stands in the way of further refinement.
2. Clients may believe that the design is finalized when more refinement is required.
3. They are expensive to produce,

WHY USE THIS METHOD?

May be used to get approval for a final design from a client or to create images for literature or a web site prior to the availability of manufactured products.

WHEN TO USE THIS METHOD

1. Explore Concepts

HOW TO USE THIS METHOD

1. They give non-designers a good idea of what the production object will look like and feel like.

REFERENCES

1. Constantine, L. L., Windl, H., Noble, J., and Lockwood, L. A. D. "From Abstraction to Realization in User Interface Design: Abstract Prototypes Based on Canonical Components." Working Paper, The Convergence Colloquy, July 2000.

361

Annex A
Templates

ACTION PLAN

ACTION PLAN:						
OBJECTIVE:						
No.	ITEM	PERSON	RESOURCE	DATE	ACTUAL	STATUS

COMPARATIVE MATRIX

	1	2	3	4	5	6	7
....							
....							
....							
....							
....							
....							
....							
....							
....							
....							
....							
....							
....							
....							
....							
....							
....							

DECISION RINGS

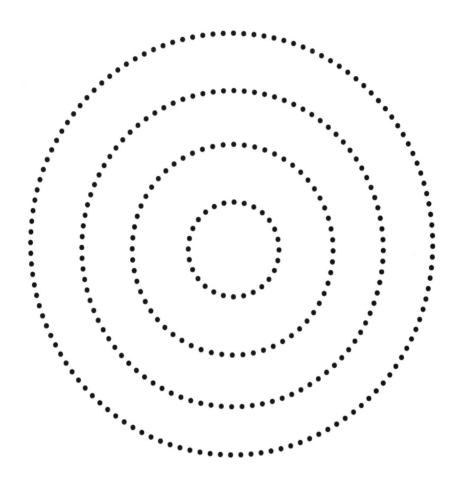

GOAL GRID

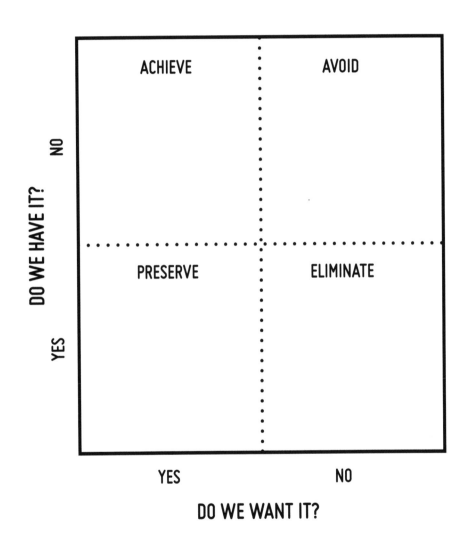

HEPTALYSIS

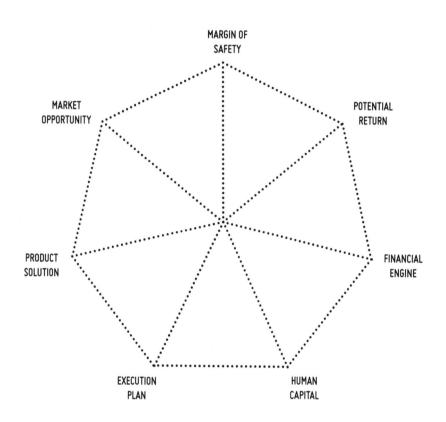

MEETING EVALUATION

	1	2	3	4	5
Meeting started on time	1	2	3	4	5
Agenda was distributed before the meeting	1	2	3	4	5
The meeting followed the agenda	1	2	3	4	5
All attendees participated	1	2	3	4	5
The meeting was an effective use of time	1	2	3	4	5
Progress was made	1	2	3	4	5
The team reached collective decisions	1	2	3	4	5
The facilitator summarized the results	1	2	3	4	5
Tasks were allocated	1	2	3	4	5
Previous meeting tasks were completed	1	2	3	4	5
The purpose of the meeting was clear	1	2	3	4	5
The meeting finished on time	1	2	3	4	5
TOTAL					

1:Very Unsatisfactory   2:Unsatisfactory   3:Average   4:Satisfactory   5 Very satisfactory

MULTIVOTING SCORE SHEET

A	B	C	D	E	F	G	H	I	J	K	L	M

N	O	P	Q	R	S	T	U	V	W	X	Y	Z

POLARITIES MATRIX

POLARITIES	++	+	0	–	– –

RISK REWARD ANALYSIS

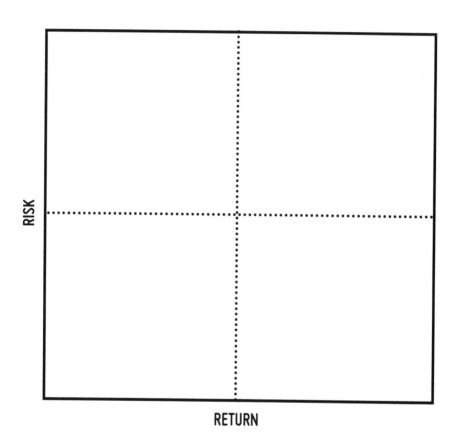

RISK MAP

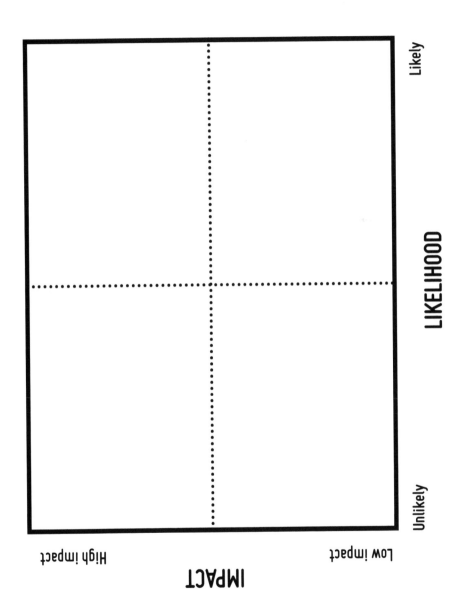

LIKELIHOOD

Likely

Unlikely

IMPACT

High impact

Low impact

REFRAMING MATRIX

DESIGN PROBLEM...
....

PRODUCT PERSPECTIVE	PLANNING PERSPECTIVE
POTENTIAL PERSPECTIVE	PEOPLE PERSPECTIVE

WORD DIAMOND

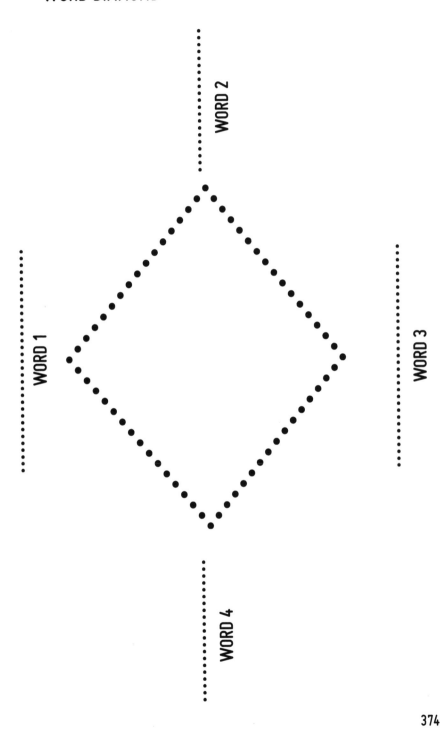

WORD 1

WORD 2

WORD 3

WORD 4

index

3p analysis 30
10 x 10 sketch method 270

A

Abhidharma 10
a/b testing 354
Abu Rayman al-Biruni 170
action plan 34, 336
active listening 128
Activity 202
activity analysis 130
Adler, Mortimer Jerome 58
Affinity diagrams 302
age 7, 11, 23, 50, 229
Aimone, L. 19, 20, 21, 22, 24, 25, 26
Alexander, Christopher Wolfgang 271
Alexander, Greg 104
alexander's method 271
Analytical thinking 3
anthropometric analysis 132
Anthropometrics 132
anthropopump 134
appreciative inquiry 35
Aristoteles 58
Arnold, John D. 66
assumption surfacing 38
attribute analysis 272
Atwater, Eastwood 128
autoethnography 136
Avison, D. 339

B

Bailey, K. 272, 300, 328
bar chart 237, 238
Barker, Richard 90
Barnard, Chester A 66
Baron, J. 56

Basadur, Min 342
Battelle Institute 116, 323
behavior 52, 134, 136, 166, 184, 194, 196,
          200, 201, 202, 203, 204, 206, 207,
          208, 228, 256, 344
Behavior 200, 201, 202, 203, 206, 207, 208
Bell Communications 359
Bengtsson, Anders 188
benjamin franklin method 276
bhag 40
blind trials: double blind trial 138
blind trials: single blind trial 137
body language 19, 20, 21, 22, 23, 24, 25, 26,
          128, 171, 179, 213, 316
Bodystorm 182
Bossard 96
Boucher 99
boundaries 72, 132, 262
boundary examination 42
Bowman, C 44
Bowman, Cliff 44
Bowman's Strategy 44
bowman's strategy clock 43, 44
Boynlon, A.C. 54
brainstorm 8, 120, 156, 240, 266, 290, 291,
          315, 329, 336, 339, 342, 346, 358
brainstorming 88, 274, 277, 278, 280, 282,
          284, 286, 288, 290, 291, 292, 294,
          296, 298, 316, 318, 323, 347, 358
          240, 274, 280, 284, 288, 291, 292,
          294, 296, 298
analogies and metaphors 274
brainstorming: greeting cards 280
brainstorming:
nominal group method 282
brainstorming: out of the box 284
brainstorming: pool 288

brainstorming: post-it 290
brainstorming: rolestorming 291
brainstorming: starbusting 292
brainstorming: stp 294
brainstorming: up and down 296
brainstorming: wishful thinking 298
brainstorms 34, 60, 66, 116, 254, 302, 308, 318
brand 3, 49
briefing checklist: product design 49
briefing checklist: web design 50
Brill, Peter L. 104
Broadbent 346
Brown, K. G. 68
Brown, Tim 4
Buchanan, Richard 4
bullet proofing 240
Burns, A. C. 214
Burns, Alvin 82
Burns, Ronald 82
Bush, R. F. 214
business matrix analysis 300
business process 78
Butler, Ava S 23, 30, 64, 118, 274, 294
Butler, Ava S. 23, 30, 64, 118, 274, 294
Button, S. B., 68

C

Carifio, James 82
Cartwright, D. 60
case studies 140, 142, 144, 146, 148, 150, 184
case studies: clinical 140
case studies: historical 142
case studies: multi case 144
case studies: observational 146
case studies: oral history 148
case studies: situational 150

case study 136, 140, 142, 144, 146, 148, 150
catwoe 92
Centre for Corporate Social Performance and Ethics 52
Chambers, R L, 223, 224, 226, 228, 229, 230, 232
Chang, Heewon. 136
Checkland, Peter 92, 339
checklist: environmentally responsible design 46
Christioan LM. 152
Clark, Charles Hutchinson. 274, 280, 284, 291, 292, 294, 296, 298
clarkson ethics principles 52
Clegg,Dai 90
clinical case study 140
close ended questions 152, 218
Cluster 302
cluster analysis 302
Cochran, William G. 223, 224, 226, 228, 229, 230, 232
Cohen, Alan 5
Collaboration 6
collective notebook 304
Collins, J 40
color 152, 260, 272, 286
communicate 52, 88, 308
communication 35, 46, 52, 100, 124, 128, 148, 213, 308, 316
comparative matrix 241, 242, 364
competencies model 306
competitors 44, 49, 50, 54, 60, 70, 98, 102, 156, 342
Cone, J. D. 184, 194
conflict 5, 66, 308, 347, 348
conjoint analysis 153, 154
consensus decision making 308

index

Constantine, L. L. 358, 360

constraints 7, 19, 20, 21, 22, 23, 24, 25, 26, 68

consumption 46

context 3, 6, 7, 13, 48, 106, 126, 130, 148, 162, 166, 170, 171, 172, 173, 174, 175, 176, 177, 178, 179, 180, 181, 182, 188, 190, 200, 201, 203, 204, 206, 207, 208, 209, 228, 278, 315, 336, 338

contextual 130

contextual interviews 130

continuous improvement 160, 342

contradiction 58

convergent thinking 306, 310, 315, 335, 342

countermeasures matrix 313, 314, 365

Crawford, C. 277

crawford slip method 277, 278

Crawford slip method 277

creative problem solving process 315, 335

critical success factor 53, 54

critical thinking 10, 11, 12, 13, 284, 288, 291, 294, 296

Critical thinking 10, 11, 14

Cropley, Arthur 310

cross-disciplinary teams 18

Cultural 5, 386

culture 7, 49, 60, 96, 142, 144, 146, 166, 186, 325

Curedale, Rob 385, 386

customer 98, 114, 156, 158, 278, 300

customer first questions 156

customer needs matrix 158

customers 35, 47, 50, 54, 70, 88, 92, 98, 156, 158, 223, 337, 342

Customers 92, 97, 109, 342

Cutler, Bob 32

D

Dalkey, Norman 244

Daniel, Ronald 54

dark horse prototype 358, 360

Daubenton, Louis-Jean-Marie 132

De bono, Edward 42

decision rings 56

Deepan Siddhu 70

DeGeest, D 68

deliverables 7, 50

Delphi Method 244

deming cycle 160

Deming Cycle 160

Deming, W. Edwards 160

design problem 68, 272, 300, 318, 328, 330, 358

Design thinking 2, 3, 4, 6, 7, 18

Design thinking process 7

Dettmer H, W. 277

De Wit 58

dialectical inquiry 58

Diffrient, Niels 132

Dillman D. 152

disassembly 46

disney method 278

disposable 46

distribution channels 49

divergent thinking 312

diversity 5, 6, 20, 100, 177

Diversity 5

Donnelly, R. A. 238

dot diagram 245, 246

double reversal 318

Dow, George 258

dramaturgy 162

drawing 164

drawing experiences 164

drawings 164, 168, 339
Duncan 136

E

ecological 46
Eisenhower 10, 30, 34, 35, 42, 43, 44, 58, 60,
          74, 80, 84, 86, 98, 104, 106, 114, 124,
          128, 130, 136, 140, 150, 156, 164,
          168, 186, 220, 240, 278, 298, 302,
          308, 318, 329, 330, 338, 343, 349,
          350, 354, 377
Eison, J.A. 68
Elder, Linda 10
Ellis, Carolyn. 136
emotion 10
Empathy 3, 5, 6, 182
employees 50, 73, 78, 88, 192, 296
end-of-life 46
energy 46
Engels 58
Ennis, Robert H. 13, 14
environmental 6, 46, 92, 99, 100
Environmental 3, 6, 92, 99, 100
Ethical 200, 220
ethnocentrism 166, 168
Execution plan 70
Execution Plan 70
explore represent share 168
eyesight 132

F

Fact finding 341
Fahey 99
Faulkner, D 44
Faulkner, David 44
feature permutation 247, 248
feedback 8, 68, 88, 170, 209, 344, 359

Fergueson, S. 19, 20, 21, 22, 24, 25, 26
Fichte 58
Fichtean Dialectics 58
field experiment 170
Fitzgerald, G. 339
Florida, Richard 4
focus group 171, 172, 173, 174, 175, 176,
          177, 178, 179, 180, 181, 209, 212
focus group: client participant 171
focus group: devil's advocate 172
focus group: dual moderator 173
focus group: mini focus group 174
focus group: online 175
focus group: other participant 176
focus group:
respondent moderator 177
focus group: structured 178
focus group: teleconference 179
focus group: unstructured 181
focus troupe 182
Foddy, W. H. 214
fog index 320
follow-up sessions 134
force field analysis 60
Fox, William 282
Franklin, Benjamin 137, 138, 276
French, John R. P. 60, 196
Friedman, L.M. 137, 138
Friedman, M. P. 202
FRISCO 13
future wheel 61, 62

G

gender, 7, 49
generative prototyping 356
Giana M. Eckhardt. 188
Gilbreth, Frank 262

index

Glenn, Jerome 62
global warming 46
goal grid 66
goal orientation 68
goals 11, 60, 66, 78, 88, 90, 91, 168, 202, 203, 204, 329, 347, 348
go and no go 64
Google 40, 354
Gordon, Thomas 128
gozinto chart 249, 250
Grabow, Stephen: 271
Graph 44, 54, 238
Graves, Tom 124
Green, Paul 154
Groarke, Leo 14
group circle 316
Groves, Robert 223, 224, 226, 228, 229, 230,
Gunning, Robert 320

H

habitat 46
Haschak, Paul G. 88
hawthorne effect 196
hearing 128, 132
Hegel 58
Hegelian dialectic 58
Helmer. Olaf 244
heptalysis 69, 70, 368
Heraclites 58
heuristic ideation 322
Hewlett-Packard 156
High fidelity prototype 5
historical 142
Human capital 70
human rights 52
humility 11
Hunt, Scott A. 162

Hurson, Tim 315, 335

I

Ice-breaker 19, 20, 21, 22, 23, 24, 25, 26
icebreaker: looking back 22
Ice breakers 18
I Ching 58
idea advocate 323
Idea finding 341
IDEO 164
idiographic approach 184
Inference 13
information market 324
innovation diagnostic 186
intellectual property 8, 49
intellectual property search 49
interview: naturalistic group 188
interviews 36, 96, 130, 140, 142, 144, 148,
150, 158, 171, 172, 173, 174, 175,
176, 177, 178, 179, 180, 181, 190,
209, 213, 214
interviews: photo elicitation 190
Isaksen 240
Ishikawa, Sara 330
is is not 72
Iteration 8

J

Javalgi, D 32
Jefferson, N.C 88
Jenkins, Gwilym 92
J. Muller, Michael 359
Johnson, James A 54
Jones, John Christopher 4, 266, 326

K

kaizen method 73
kalama sutta 10
Kant 58
Kellermann, P. 344
Kelley, W. M. 238
Kendrick, Tom 72
Kepner 76, 240
Kepner, Charles 76
kepner tregoe analysis 76
key performance indicator 78
Key performance indicators 78
kick off meeting 80
Klein, Gary 106

L

Lao Tzu 58
Laplace, Pierre Simon 223, 224, 226, 228, 229, 230, 232
Laraia, Anthony C. 73
Lavoisier, Antoine 137, 138
leadership 68, 96, 347, 348
Leadership 347, 348
Lego 192, 356
Le Play, Frederic 140, 142, 144, 146, 148, 150
Levitt, Steven D. 196
Lewin, Kurt 60
life cycle 46, 264
Liker, Jeffrey 73
Likert, Rensis 82
likert scale 82
Linde, Frank 324
Lind, James 220
line chart 251, 252
linking diagram 253, 254
List, John A. 196
Lloyd, G. 316
location 25, 49, 80

Lockwood, L. A. D. 358, 360
Louviere, Jordan 154

M

Malinowski, Bronisław 201, 204, 206
Management 52, 54, 109, 110, 116, 198, 253, 264, 350, 356
Managers 52
manufacture 49
manufacturing 49, 253
Maréchal, Garance 136
Margin of safety 70
market 43, 46, 50, 53, 70, 100, 241, 253, 300, 324, 337
marketing 32, 50, 99, 256, 337
marketing mix 32
market opportunities 46
Market opportunity 70
Market Opportunity. 70
Martin, Roger 4
Marx 58
Maslow, Abraham 256
maslow's hierarchy 255, 256
Mason, Richard O 38
Matchett, Edward 325
matchett's
fundamental design method 325
Mathieu, J. E. 68
matrix 38, 54, 102, 158, 242, 271, 272, 300, 314, 328, 338
Maurer, Robert 73
Mayo, Elton 196
McFadzean, E. 322
McFadzean, Elspeth 198, 349, 350
McGahan, A. M. 122
McGahan, Anita M. 122
McGinis, Vern 88

index

McKinsey & Company 54
Mead, Margaret 201, 204, 206
meaning 10, 14, 42, 128, 190, 194, 208, 258
Mecca 99
meeting evaluation 84
Meier, David 73
Merton, Robert K. 171, 172, 173, 174, 175,
    176, 177, 178, 180, 181
method bank 192
Meyer 58
mirror 86, 171, 172, 173, 174, 175, 176, 177,
    178, 179, 180, 181
mission statement 40, 88
Misuse 182
Misuse scenarios 182
Moger, Susan 74
Monk, A. F. 339
Moore, Geoffrey 264
moral 52, 124
Morgan, Michael 338
morphological analysis 328
Morrison 99
moscow prioritization 90
Mosley, J. 316
most analysis 91
Munn, P. 316

N

Narayanan 99
nature 36, 46, 211, 347
need 48, 49, 54, 68, 92, 98, 132, 152, 182,
    210, 256, 288, 294, 315, 336
Need 6, 7, 49, 182, 288
needs 5, 6, 18, 40, 46, 54, 64, 68, 73, 98, 100,
    156, 158, 159, 162, 256, 300, 342,
    354, 356
Nickols, Fred 66

Noble, J. 358, 360
Nokia 40, 386
nomothetic approach 194
Norris, K.W. 272, 300, 328

O

objectives 8, 50, 66, 76, 80, 124, 160, 200,
    201, 206, 207, 312
object stimulation 198
O'Brien, Denis 168
observation 200, 201, 202, 206, 207
observation: covert 200
observation: direct 201
observation: indirect 202
observation: non participant 203
observation: overt 206
observation: participant 204
observation: structured 207
Observe 7, 130, 182, 201, 202, 203
octagon 96
ohmae 3c model 98
Ohmae, K. 98
online methods 209, 210, 211, 212, 213, 214,
    215, 216
online methods: clinical trials 211
online methods: ethnography 210
online methods: experiments 215
online methods: focus groups 212
online methods: interviews 213
online methods: online ethics 216
online methods: questionnaires 214
open ended questions 152, 218
Orme, B. 154
Osborn, Alex Faickney 288, 292, 296
outcomes 49, 50, 62, 64, 68, 118, 160, 166,
    220, 254, 274, 298, 324, 336

P

Page, J.K. 329
page's strategy 329
participatory design 130, 359
pattern language 330
Paul, Richard 10
Paul, Richard W. 10, 11, 12
Pearson, Karl 354
pearson's method 332
percentile 132
performance 7, 46, 73, 78, 86, 234, 264
permission 203, 204
pestel analysis 99
Peterson, Leighton 210
Pheasant, Stephen 132
phillips 66 method 334
Phillips, Donald 334
photographs 190, 266
Piaget 184
Pickens, James 280
pictogram 258
pie chart 260
pin cards 286
Pinto, R. C. 58
placebo controlled study 220
Plato 58
Point of view 6
polarities matrix 102
pollution 46
Porras, J 40
Porte 99
Potential return 70
powergram 104
premortem 106
Problem definition 341
Problem finding 341
process flow diagram 262

P

product 5, 8, 32, 44, 46, 49, 70, 99, 132, 154,
        156, 158, 182, 248, 250, 264, 266,
        325, 337, 339, 360, 386
Product 5, 8, 49, 70, 248, 264, 266, 386
productive thinking model 335
product life cycle map 264
prototype 5, 8, 182, 358, 359, 360
prototyped 48
prototypes 5, 8, 134, 170, 182, 356, 358, 359,

Q

qualitative 7, 78, 110, 186, 310
quantitative 7, 78, 110, 136, 186, 310
questionnaire 214, 216, 242
Questionnaires 120, 152, 154, 216

R

Radcliff-Brown 201, 204, 206
Rajshekhar, G 32
RAND Corporation 244
Rawlinson J. Geoffrey 274, 280, 284, 291, 292,
        294, 296, 298
Reali 306
reality check 47, 298
Recruit participants 171, 172, 173, 174, 175,
        176, 177, 178, 179, 180, 181
recyclable 48
recycled 46
Reed, Warren H. 128
reframing matrix 338
reframing the problem 74
Regulatory bodies 100
Reips, U.-D. 216
Renfro 99
requirements catalog 108
Rescher, Nicholas 244
research goals 202, 203, 204

index

responsibilities 52, 80, 104, 124
responsible 46
Richard O. Mason 38
rich pictures 339
Rickards, Tudor 74
risk map 109, 110, 373
risk reward analysis 111, 112, 372
risks 5, 7, 48, 52, 76, 110, 204, 240, 278, 310
Robert, Benford D 162
Robert H. Ennis 13, 14
Rockart, John F. 54
Roethlisberger, Fritz 196
Rogers, Carl 128
Roos, J. 356
Roos, Johan 356
rotating roles 114
Rother, Mike 160
Rowe, Peter 3
Rumelt, R. 122
Runco, Mark A 74

S

Saaksvuori, Antti 264
sampling 222, 223, 224, 226, 228, 229, 230,
Sampling 223, 224, 226, 228, 229, 230, 232
sampling: cluster 222
sampling: convenience 223
sampling: expert 226
sampling: situation 228
sampling: stratified 229
sampling: systematic 230
sampling: time 232
Sanders, Liz 356
Scenarios 7, 182
schedule 50, 80, 110
Schnelle, Wolfgang 286
Scope 7

Secondary research 7
secret ballot 94
secret voting 340
Seglin, Jeffrey L. 52
semantic intuition 116
service 8, 46, 53, 70, 100, 154, 156, 158, 182,
    266, 272, 337, 339
Services 5
seven p's 32
Shewhart cycle. 160
shredded questions 118
Silberman, Mel 120
Silverstein, Murray 330
simple 5, 19, 20, 21, 22, 23, 24, 25, 26, 30, 48,
    152, 218, 229, 230, 238, 248, 270,
    276, 356, 359
simplex method 341
simplex problem solving 342
Sisco, B. R. 19, 20, 21, 22, 24, 25, 26
sketch 248, 270, 286
Skinner, C J 223, 224, 226, 228, 229, 230, 232
small groups 343
Smyth J 152
Sobocan, Jan 14
sociodrama 344
sociogram 233, 234
Socrates 10, 58
Socratic 12, 58
Socratic discussion 12
Srinivasan, V. 154
Srinivasan, V. "Seenu" 154
Stakeholder 52, 100
stakeholders 7, 8, 47, 48, 52, 60, 72, 80, 88,
    92, 96, 104, 120, 124, 162, 171, 172,
    173, 174, 175, 176, 177, 178, 179,
    180, 181, 186, 304, 315, 332, 336,
    338

stakeholder scope map 120
Stake, Robert E. 140, 142, 144, 146, 148, 150
Stanford University 154, 358
Statler, M. 356
Sternberg, Robert J. 348
Stock, Wolfgang G. 324
Strategic 386
strategies 44, 46, 68, 91, 98, 110, 325, 326, 346
strategy 7, 44, 49, 60, 70, 91, 92, 98, 110, 122, 186, 234, 278, 329, 337, 346, 359
strategy switching 346
structure 66, 100, 104, 213, 234, 310
structured 36, 38, 168, 178, 207, 310, 347,
style 96, 212, 272, 347, 348
Success Factors 54
Sustainability 100

T

Tague, Nancy R. 286
Tasks 19, 20, 21, 22, 23, 24, 25, 26, 213
team based design 18
team building exercises 18
test 5, 8, 137, 138, 160, 170, 196, 200, 201, 206, 207, 312
testing 47, 76, 209, 354, 359
Tew, M. 316
The Matchett Foundation 326
Thinkering 356
Tilley, Alvin R. 132
toxic 46
Toyota 73, 160
trajectories of change 122
Treffinger 240
Tregoe 76, 240
Tregoe, Benjamin 76

Tufte, E. 56

U

Unstructured 64, 118, 274
user needs 356

V

VanGundy 322, 350
Vazsonyi, A. 250
Vickers, Geoffrey 35
Victor, B. 356
Victor, Bart 356
visual dissonance 266
Vote 94
vpec-t 124
Vroom, Victor H. 348
vroom yetton decision model 347

W

Warfield, J. N. 116
web site 360
Weiss, Joseph W. 52
Wilson, Edith 156
Wilson, R. W. 202
Wilson, Samuel M. 210
Winans, William 32
Windl, H. 358, 360
word diamond 349, 350, 377

Y

Yetton, Phillip W. 348

Z

Zajac, D. M. 68
Zechmeister, John J. 201, 202, 203, 206, 207,
Zwicky, Fritz 272, 300, 328

other titles in the design methods series

Design Methods 1
200 ways to apply design thinking

Author: Robert A Curedale
Published by:
Design Community College Inc.
PO Box 1153
Topanga CA 90290 USA

Edition 1 November 2012

ISBN-10:0988236206
ISBN-13:978-0-9882362-0-2

The Design Thinking Manual

Author: Robert A Curedale
Published by:
Design Community College Inc.
PO Box 1153
Topanga CA 90290 USA

Edition 1 January 2013

ISBN-10: 0988236214
ISBN-13: 978-0-9882362-1-9

Structured Workshops

The author presents workshops online and in person in global locations for executives, engineers, designers, technology professionals and anyone interested in learning and applying these proven innovation methods. For information contact: info@curedale.com

about the author

Rob Curedale was born in Australia and worked as a designer, director and educator in leading design offices in London, Sydney, Switzerland, Portugal, Los Angeles, Silicon Valley, Detroit, and China. He designed and managed over 1,000 products and experiences as a consultant and in-house design leader for the world's most respected brands. Rob has three decades experience in every aspect of product development, leading design teams to achieve transformational improvements in operating and financial results. He has extensive experience in forging strategic growth, competitive advantage, and a background in expanding business into emerging markets through user advocacy and extensive cross cultural expertise. Rob's designs can be found in millions of homes and workplaces around the world.

Rob works currently as a Adjunct Professor at Art Center College of Design in Pasadena and consults to organizations in the United States and internationally and presents workshops related to design. He has taught as a member of staff and presented lectures and workshops at many respected design schools and universities throughout the world including Yale, Pepperdine University, Art Center Pasadena, Loyola University, Cranbrook, Pratt, Art Center Europe; a faculty member at SCA and UTS Sydney; as Chair of Product Design and Furniture Design at the College for Creative Studies in Detroit, then the largest product design school in North America, Art Institute Hollywood, Cal State San Jose, Escola De Artes e Design in Oporto Portugal, Instituto De Artes Visuals, Design e Marketing, Lisbon, Southern Yangtze University, Jiao Tong University in Shanghai and Nanjing Arts Institute in China.

Rob's design practice experience includes projects for HP, Philips, GEC, Nokia, Sun, Apple, Canon, Motorola, Nissan, Audi VW, Disney, RTKL, Governments of the UAE,UK, Australia, Steelcase, Hon, Castelli, Hamilton Medical, Zyliss, Belkin, Gensler, Haworth, Honeywell, NEC, Hoover, Packard Bell, Dell, Black & Decker, Coleman and Harmon Kardon. Categories including furniture, healthcare, consumer electronics, sporting, homewares, military, exhibits, packaging. His products and experiences can be found in millions of homes and businesses throughout the world.

Rob established and manages the largest network of designers and architects in the world with more than 300,000 professional members working in every field of design.